248.89
Sm 6

Nurturing the Soul
of the Youth Worker

by
Tim Smith

Foreword by Jim Burns

Nyack College Library

Loveland, Colorado

Nurturing the Soul of the Youth Worker

Copyright © 1999 Tim D. Smith

All rights reserved. No part of this book may be reproduced in any manner whatsoever without prior written permission from the publisher, except where noted in the text and in the case of brief quotations embodied in critical articles and reviews. For information write Permissions, Group Publishing, Inc., Dept. PD, P.O. Box 481, Loveland, CO 80539.

Visit our Web site: **www.grouppublishing.com**

Credits
Editor: Amy Simpson
Creative Development Editor: Jim Kochenburger
Chief Creative Officer: Joani Schultz
Copy Editor: Alison Imbriaco
Art Director: Kari K. Monson
Cover Art Director/Designer: Jeff A. Storm
Computer Graphic Artist: Joyce Douglas
Illustrator: Dave Klug
Cover Photographer: Tony Stone Images
Production Manager: Alexander Jorgensen

Unless otherwise noted, Scripture taken from the HOLY BIBLE, NEW INTERNATIONAL VERSION. Copyright © 1973, 1978, 1984 by International Bible Society. Used by permission of Zondervan Publishing House. All rights reserved.

Library of Congress Cataloging-in-Publication Data
Smith, Tim, 1954-
    Nurturing the soul of the youth worker / by Tim Smith ; foreword
by Jim Burns.
      p. cm.
    Includes bibliographical references (p.) .
    ISBN 0-7644-2135-2
    1. Church youth workers. 2. Christian leadership. 3. Church work
with youth. I. Title.
BV4447.S6345 1999
248.8'9--dc21   99-36408
                                                        CIP

10 9 8 7 6 5 4 3 2 1   08 07 06 05 04 03 02 01 00 99

Printed in the United States of America.

What People Are Saying About
Nurturing the Soul of the Youth Worker
by Tim Smith

"Nurturing the Soul of the Youth Worker is refreshingly new material. It's very much a holistic approach to reaching and ministering to kids. The focus on the inner life of the youth worker is wonderful. All of us in youth work need this book."

Jim Burns

President

National Institute of Youth Ministry

author of *Youth Builder*

"A much needed blueprint for developing character in the life of the youth worker, *Nurturing the Soul of the Youth Worker*, offers a fresh, practical, and biblical strategy to develop leaders with integrity. Tim Smith reminds us that effective youth ministry is not simply creativity and skill, but an issue of the heart. If you have a passion for youth and God, read this book."

Dr. Barry St. Clair

Reach Out Youth Solutions

"Too many of us live and work on the outer edges of ministry—where the programs, activities, events, lessons, and "hot ideas" are found. But, as with riding a merry-go-round, one must move toward the center to avoid falling off. Here Tim Smith identifies core principles that are central to effective youth ministry and recommends a practical approach to nurturing your soul. You won't find quick fixes and simple solutions to the thorny challenges of youth ministry here, but you will find the kind of wisdom that can keep you on the merry-go-round of youth ministry for many years to come. I enthusiastically recommend this book!"

Wayne Rice

Understanding Your Teenager

"Nurturing the Soul of the Youth Worker is a gold mine of wisdom for rookies and veteran youth leaders. There are nuggets of passion and insight and pearls of life-giving principles. It's one book that you need to read. It could revolutionize your entire life."

Dr. David Olshine

Chairman of Youth Ministry

Columbia International University

Columbia, South Carolina

"In a world where many youth workers get caught in the performance trap of bigger and better, *Nurturing the Soul of the Youth Worker* calls youth work back to its basics—back to the things which will really make youth ministry effective—<u>and that is</u> the heart, the mind, and the spirit of the youth worker. This is not a book of how-to's, it is a book of character and integrity and a book that calls us to be the people of God. This book is "must" reading for any youth worker."

Dr. Ridge Burns
Executive Director
Forest Home Christian Conference Center

"Tim has written just what my volunteer leaders need to read. This material is fresh and readable, and, best of all, these are the principles that *work*. Pastors need to get a copy of this into the hands of everyone working with the teens in their church!"

Dr. Daniel Hahn
Pastor of Students and Families
Mission Hills Church
Professor of Youth Ministry
Talbot School of Theology

"The principles of nurturing the soul are not meant to be tricks of the trade, but building blocks of character, passion, and effectiveness that will lay a firm foundation for solid ministry. I like the emphasis on the soul and believe that it has been a forgotten topic in youth ministry. I also appreciate Tim Smith's emphasis on making youth ministry family-friendly."

Chap Clark, Ph.D.
Associate Professor of Youth and Family Ministries
Fuller Theological Seminary

"Today's teenagers are not crying out for more slick youth ministry programs but they are desperate for caring people in their life. This book answers their desperation by pointing youth workers toward developing souls that are healthy, nurtured, and passionate for God. This book isn't full of creative ideas and fancy programs, but it is full of proven steps in the journey of becoming God's person."

Doug Fields
Youth Pastor, Saddleback Church
author of *Purpose Driven Youth Ministry*

Dedication

Dedicated to Roman Sanchez and Mike Katzenberger
for all the soul they put into our youth ministry.

Tim Smith is available for consulting and speaking on youth and family issues.
Contact him at
P.O. Box 7736
Thousand Oaks, CA 91360
or at
tdwrdsmith@aol.com

Other Books by Tim Smith

Almost Cool. Chicago, IL: Moody Press, 1997. A helpful handbook written for parents of teenagers.

Family Sunday School Fun. Loveland, CO: Group Publishing, Inc., 1999. A collection of Bible lessons for children and parents.

Hi. I'm Bob and I'm the Parent of a Teenager. Ventura, CA: Gospel Light, 1991. A guide to beginning and leading a support group for parents of teens.

Contents

Foreword

I had just walked off the stage at what the sponsors called one of the largest youth events ever held in their state. The music had been wonderful. The spirit of excitement in the crowd was electric. I believe I felt God's spirit in my message, and the response to a call to commitment was absolutely overwhelming. What a night!

The wife of an old friend came right up to me afterwards. Her husband had been a spiritual mentor in my life, and he had recently had to leave his position of leadership because of sexual immorality. She gave me a hug, and, with tears in her eyes, she said, "Jim, untended fires soon become nothing but a pile of ashes."

Her words threw me. I had expected "Isn't God wonderful?" or "Good job." Instead, I got *"Untended fires soon become nothing but a pile of ashes."*

My friend had experienced the same youth event I had. She had seen the excitement of the kids. She had watched the intense response of the students as they made beautiful commitments to our Lord Jesus Christ. But frankly, she had been there before. Hers and her husband's lifework had been to serve Jesus, and, for most of their years, the couple had experienced phenomenal fruit in the area of youth ministry. She also knew firsthand the depth of pain of a broken relationship, sin, and failure in the ministry. In a sense she had experienced "the thrill of victory and the agony of defeat."

Now she was approaching me with what I believe was a word from God: *Untended fires soon become nothing but a pile of ashes.*

As I read Tim Smith's wonderful book, I couldn't help but think back to the days of very few youth ministry resources and only a handful of "professional" youth workers. They were days with no youth ministry magazines, few conferences, little training, and a lot of prayer. Those who chose youth work were the weird ones. (Perhaps they still are today!) I look at those times as a season of burning desire to reach students with the gospel of Jesus Christ. We would do anything to get their attention. I remember swallowing goldfish and shaving my beard just to get students out to an event! Needless to say, the programs have changed; we have quality resources, and the training is outstanding.

It's a new millennium of youth work with new problems and changing issues. *Nurturing the Soul of the Youth Worker* is one of the first books to be written for youth work in the new millennium. It's very much a holistic approach to reaching and ministering to kids. The focus on the inner life of the youth worker is wonderful. Tim is helping youth workers see that untended fires soon become nothing but a pile of ashes.

In case you haven't had the privilege of meeting Tim Smith, he is an exceptional leader on the cutting edge of youth and family ministry. He knows what he is talking about and is ministering today in a fresh new format. Tim's approach to family ministry, culture, team ministry, and administration is refreshingly fresh material.

It was a joy to read this book. I know it will nurture your soul as you walk the path Tim takes you on. All of us in youth work need this book. Youth ministry is one of the most exciting and influential areas of the church, and we must have healthy souls in order to face the daily battle for the lives of our kids. Thank you for your commitment to student ministry, and thank God for people such as you who are influencing more students for eternity than you ever will imagine.

Jim Burns
President
National Institute of Youth Ministry
Author of *Youth Builder*

A Passion for Souls

"**W**hat lies behind us and what lies before us are tiny matters compared to what lies within us."—*Oliver Wendell Holmes*

Within the soul of every youth worker is a passion for kids—a passion to make a significant and lasting impact on each one of them. More than a "liking to work with" kids, this passion is an intense desire for influence. If all we wanted was to hang around adolescents, we could take up snowboarding. But what drives us who minister to youth is the hope that we might be able to benefit individual teenagers and change the world for the kingdom of Christ. We don't simply want to see teenagers come to our youth group, we want to touch their souls.

It is this passion for souls that will bring about a renaissance in youth ministry as we launch into a new millennium. Ours is an era of cataclysmic change—old walls are knocked down, new ones are erected. Some people are liberated, while poverty, violence, famine, and religious fanaticism hold others hostage.

It's within this environment that we seek to minister. In the sixties we witnessed the explosion of the "rally and big event" youth ministry. In the seventies we experienced the Jesus movement and the growth of worship and small group Bible study. In the eighties we observed much emphasis on church growth and the "bigger is better" (quantity) mentality in youth work. In the nineties we saw a concern for quality in youth ministry. The economics of the decade and the crisis within the culture demanded that we produce quality. But the focus was mainly on *image* and *perception*.

Now as we begin the first decade in a new millennium, we need quality from the inside out. We need to nurture the souls of our youth. And the best place to begin is with the nurturing of our own souls. Perhaps if our teenagers see us nurturing our own souls, they'll understand that such nurture is important for them as well.

The Family in Crisis

The need for a caring, coherent youth ministry has never been greater. Youth culture has become increasingly violent. Fifteen-year-old students are bringing automatic weapons to school and gunning down their peers and teachers. It's risky to be a teenager today. Just being at school at the wrong time could get you shot.

Many teenagers are disillusioned. They feel that adults have let them down. Their own parents have let them down and let each other down.

The near disappearance of marriage as a dependable, permanent structure within which children can live out their childhood is surely the most consequential change that has occurred in the last two decades. [1]

One reason that divorce can be so traumatic is that the breakup of the family often confuses roles. The teenager may have to act like a parent and assume responsibility because the parent is acting like a child. The issues of rejection, desertion, separation, and loss have an incredible impact on the parent as well as the teenager. In time, the parent may recover, but the adolescent will never be the same—innocence will never be recaptured. Teenagers who have experienced the wages and burden of divorce may be frightened by what they saw. Children of divorce discover that their parents are often as helpless, confused, and vulnerable as they are. In the quiet, dark hours they may lie awake and worry, "Who will take care of me if my parents can't even take care of themselves?"

As a result of family breakup, a teenager becomes more vulnerable to the stresses of modern life.

Statistically, children of divorce are more likely to become involved with alcohol and drugs, to commit suicide, to get in trouble with the law, to fail in school. As time goes on, we're discovering new and troubling connections between the children of divorce and a host of grave social problems, from runaways to sexual abuse and even mass hysteria.[2] Clearly, the instability of the family in our culture is damaging young people. And not just the children of divorce. The pain felt by children of divorce permeates our culture.

Dynamic new-millennium youth ministry looks at teenagers environmentally. It asks such questions as "What kind of environment does she live in?" and "What kind of emotional climate does he go home to?" Gone are the days when we could deal with the teenager as an individual with no regard for his or her environment. We need to do EIRs (Environmental Impact Reports) on our teenagers to discover the systems they live in.

An ecological approach to youth ministry will prepare us to face the crisis in our culture. Creating windows into the souls of our kids will help us genuinely understand what lies within them.

A Commitment to Character

We can't afford the luxury of playing around with youth ministry anymore. We need to work at it. A cosmetic approach that deals with such externals as numbers, dollars, and celebrities won't cut it in a world of chaos and change. These become tiny matters when we look at the core issues—the matters of the heart.

In a culture that's drowning in a deluge of voices and information, it's character that communicates most effectively. As Ralph Waldo Emerson said, "What you are shouts so loudly in my ears I cannot hear what you say." What we *are* communicates more eloquently than anything we *say* or *do*.

Youth ministry used to mean focusing on the young person as an individual, entertaining him or her a little, and then slipping in a little something about God. It's all changed—the stakes are much higher. Teenagers are more fragile, they're more susceptible to stress, and they now face an array of risky behavior choices.

We need to build into them a commitment to character growth—growth from the inside out. The best way to begin this kind of growth is to model it ourselves.

"The Character Ethic is based on the fundamental idea that there are *principles* that govern human effectiveness—natural laws in the human dimension that are just as real, just as unchanging, and, arguably, just as 'there' as laws such as gravity are in the physical dimension."[3]

The *principles* of life-changing youth ministry are different from the *practices* that are culturally, demographically, or situationally specific. In other words, while practices may work in Boise but fail in Boston, principles are proven, fundamental truths that have universal application. Principles are transferable from situation to situation. If a principle is true, it will be effective in Boise *and* Boston.

When principles are integrated into a person's thinking, they begin to shape that person's character. In time, the principles develop into habits, and these habits are the behaviors that nurture the soul. Our goal, then, is to nurture our souls by studying the habits of effective youth workers and integrating timeless truths into our thinking. If we have principles, we'll have clear and permanent guidelines on our journey toward powerful and lasting youth ministry.

An Introduction to *Nurturing the Soul of the Youth Worker*

"Nurture" can be defined as "anything that nourishes; food." In order to nourish our souls, we need to identify those basic food groups that can provide the nourishment we need. So far, I've identified eight sources of nutrition for a healthy soul.

1. Nurture your soul with **a commitment to lifelong learning.**

Approaching life as a learner, rather than a teacher, creates the perspective necessary for growth. If we're learners, we interpret all life's situations and experiences as opportunities for learning and personal involvement.

A few years ago, I went with Peter, my coworker in youth ministry, to a national convention for youth workers in San Francisco. In the lobby, we met a youth pastor from Texas who wanted a tour of San Francisco. He had the rented car, and we knew San Francisco (well—at least, we knew San Francisco better than he did!). As he pulled out of the hotel parking lot, he asked,

"How big is your church?"

"About fifteen hundred on Sundays." Peter replied.

"Do you have a large youth group?" inquired Tex.

"No, not really. We only have about twenty committed kids." I explained.

This response was a strategy Peter and I had decided on because we were getting tired of "group envy," which often is rampant at youth worker conventions. We decided this "canned" response would focus on the heart of youth ministry, not the height or weight of our group. We agreed to say, "twenty committed kids," and see what responses we got. Tex fell right into it.

"Well, in Blue Rock, we have a membership of four thousand, youth membership around one thousand, a bus ministry, twenty-two buses, a full-time bus mechanic, a Christian school, a gymnasium (which we call a family center), and a new sanctuary that will seat one thousand," bragged Tex as he drove down Market Street, soaking in the city's exotic smells and sights.

Tex continued his tall tale of pastoral bravado all the way through our authentic Chinese meal in authentic Chinatown. When he excused himself to use the "little cowboys' room," Peter and I toyed with the idea of ditching him right there in Chinatown; but, we reminded ourselves, we *were* at a Christian convention. It might be hard to face him later, especially if Tony Campolo preached on compassion and ethics!

Tex reminds me that learners are listeners. He didn't listen to us the whole evening. If he asked a question, it was only to introduce a discourse on what he was doing, which was infinitely superior (at least by his account).

Peter and I were struggling with our youth group. At the time, we really could have used a good listener, or even a creative problem solver. Instead, we found ourselves trapped in a cheap rental car with a person whose mouth was stuck in the gear of self-promotion. It was a sad evening. Instead of being an opportunity to exchange ideas, support and encourage each other, and learn, it was a night of empty rhetoric, disrespect, and, on top of it all, bad sweet-and-sour pork!

A year later at the same convention, I heard someone talking about the "scandal" at Blue Rock. "What happened there?" I inquired.

"Tex was fired. He had an affair with one of the girls in his high school group. His wife is divorcing him, too," I was told.

I wasn't surprised. My impression was that Tex was a talker, not a learner. Yet he obviously needed to learn at that San Francisco convention. Sometimes I wonder if he was struggling that year, too.

2. Nurture your soul with **service.**

We lead best when we seek the welfare of those we lead, when we seek to serve rather than to be served. This was the secret of Christ's impact: "The greatest among you will be your servant" (Matthew 23:11).

An influential youth worker never forgets that he or she is in a service career. We're here to understand the needs of the customer and to be responsive to those needs. Like a good waiter or a caring shepherd, a competent youth worker anticipates needs and seizes the opportunity to minister to those in need.

Sometimes we forget the metaphor of servant leadership and buy into the corporate perception of leadership, which is based on position and power. We become obsessed with leading a large group and ministering to the masses. At these times we need to learn from the Master, who, even though he spoke to thousands, took time to

- bless a young boy who shared his lunch,
- heal a bleeding woman,
- bring a little girl back to life,
- talk to a tax collector in a tree,
- heal a blind man.

These people weren't the politically correct people of his culture. They were average "nobodies," not the "movers and shakers" of Palestine.

Jesus was service-oriented because he understood his mission. He was able to focus on the individual because he respected each person. That focus on the individual is what the parable of the lost sheep is all about. Loving youth workers don't forget about the lost sheep, even though they may have ninety-nine in the fold. Maybe that's what Dag Hammarskjold, past secretary-general of the United Nations, had in mind when he said, "It is more noble to give yourself completely to one individual than to labor diligently for the salvation of the masses."

People who lead lives that have an impact on others know the value of personal service and commitment to the individual.

3. Nurture your soul by **radiating the positive power of the Holy Spirit.**

Much of what we read in management books is about "being positive" or the right use of power. I've often read these passages and thought, "Sometimes I just don't feel like being positive. Sometimes I want to grab as much power as I can!"

Being a continually positive leader who never abuses his or her position is not only difficult—it's impossible! An attempt to minister effectively using the tools of our culture is destined to failure. To minister effectively, we need to depend completely on the Holy Spirit. Our natural gifts and abilities will synergize with our spiritual gifts to provide us with the tools we need to impact youth for Christ's kingdom.

The good news is that this ministry doesn't depend on our strengths to be effective. In fact, I often have the most significant times of ministry when I'm tired or perplexed.

" 'My grace is sufficient for you, for my power is made perfect in weakness.' Therefore I will boast all the more gladly about my weaknesses, so that Christ's power may rest on me. That is why, for Christ's sake, I delight in weaknesses, in insults, in hardships, in persecutions, in difficulties. For when I am weak, then I am strong" (2 Corinthians 12:9-10).

Christ's power can be made perfect in my weakness. In fact, I can boast of my weaknesses to create more of a vacuum for Christ's power! Now that's a deal!

4. Nurture your soul by **believing in others (and their growth).**

A few years ago, I worked with my staff to help them "expect the best from the people you lead." That effort got me in trouble. We planned a large event and recruited several capable volunteers. After we developed an overall strategy for the event together, I asked my staff to develop the specifics. Staff members discussed the event with their volunteers and decided to make changes and improvements. I gave them the freedom to do this because I trusted them and because they're the ones who know the ministry best.

The new plans upset one of the church elders. "It doesn't sound like what we thought it was going to be. Tell them to change it! Why didn't you check on them and keep this from getting out of hand?"

"Because I trust them to develop the best possible event for the kids—they're experts, and I have confidence in them. This plan is better. We'll stick with it."

My response was risky, but it paid off. Minutes later one of the leaders confided, "I've observed that you operate from a position of trust. Elder Ernie operates from a position of distrust. Now I know why people like to work with you."

I was delighted to see that my efforts to offer others my confidence and to build on their strengths and minimize their weaknesses actually made a difference.

5. Nurture your soul by **leading a balanced life.**

In rock climbing, surfing, and youth ministry, balance is crucial. It seems to me that most problems we encounter in youth ministry come from the extremes. Mature and effective youth workers have learned to balance competing demands.

The ability to say "no" is essential for a balanced youth ministry. If we say "yes" to every opportunity, the pressing urgencies we create will erode our time. I have a rule of thumb: Try to say "no" to something every day. It's liberating and quite fun once you get into it.

One day a pastor on our staff asked me if I'd help with the Day of Prayer. He offered a few reasons why he thought I should help plan it. I said, "No, thanks, I'm already doing some other extra projects." It felt great!

He responded, "OK, I'll ask Gordy if he'd like to help."

No pain, no guilt.

Youth workers with balance have committed to make skillful use of their time and their time-focus. They're able to balance their focus between the past, the present, and the future. They're willing to learn from the past and control their present in order to have an impact on their future.

Balance also has to do with an awareness of one's strengths and weaknesses. Balanced leaders aren't perfect, but they've discovered ways to capitalize on their strengths and compensate for their weaknesses.

Have you noticed that people you like to spend time with are able to laugh at themselves? A sense of humor is a trait of a balanced life. Humor is common in youth workers, but many times it's cynical, sarcastic, or demeaning. It's humor with a sting. Humor that enables us to laugh at ourselves is healthier and less risky. I'm not advocating putting yourself down; I'm suggesting that you use your own life as a source of humor—if you do, you'll never run out of material!

6. Nurture your soul by **seeing life as an adventure.**

Capable youth workers are more than lifelong learners. They're adventurers on a safari to jungles unknown. They're risk-takers who know that life is a mission that demands taking expeditions into new and uncharted territories. If comfort, stability, and security are your aspirations, then get out of youth ministry. Flexibility, change, and risk are what you're more likely to encounter in the youth ministry jungle.

True security comes from within, not from without. Inner security doesn't require the illusion of certainty or predictability that comes from categorizing or stereotyping life. Anyone who truly knows adolescents knows to give up any notions of predictability.

If we see life as an adventure, we have a perspective that allows us to experience what Christ was discussing in John 10:10b: "I have come that they may have life, and have it to the full."

Adventure-minded leaders are eager to learn from every teenager they encounter. They don't categorize them according to externals or their past. They see within each teenager the potential to live life to the fullest in Christ and to join the adventure of pursuing God's kingdom.

7. Nurture your soul with **teamwork and synergy.**

"Synergy is the state in which the whole is more than the sum of the parts."[4]

Synergistic youth ministry affirms the value and contribution of each individual. A youth worker who understands synergy will be able to make students and staff feel valuable by affirming their individual contributions and uniqueness. He or she also will be able to show individuals how their contributions and giftedness benefit the whole group. As each person feels valued, affirmed, and meaningful, a spirit of teamwork begins to develop. This esprit de corps is a result of relationship, relevance, and rallying people together. Synergy can't be forced, contrived, or manufactured—it must be grown. As it grows, it begins to take on a life of its own. This life is energy produced by the cooperative spirit of people working together effectively.

Synergy is a modern word for a concept that is two thousand years old: "If you have any encouragement from being united with Christ, if any comfort from his love, if any fellowship with the Spirit, if any tenderness and compassion, then make my joy complete by being like-minded, having the same love, being one in spirit and purpose. Do nothing out of selfish ambition or vain conceit, but in humility consider others better than yourselves. Each of you should look not only to your own interests, but also to the interests of others" (Philippians 2:1-4).

Youth workers with an understanding of synergy find it easier to recruit volunteers because people are seeking the encouragement, the love, and the focused fellowship that come as a result of spiritual teamwork.

8. Nurture your soul with a **commitment to personal renewal.**

Anyone who has been in youth work knows that ministry drains energy and passion. To be continually effective, youth workers need a strategy for personal renewal. We need to know what it is in our work that drains us. We need to recognize symptoms of fatigue and have a standard for evaluating just how worn out we really are.

Youth work is more passion than profession. If we're drained physically, emotionally, or spiritually, all the degrees on the wall won't help us shepherd our kids. It's crucial that a youth worker have times and places of renewal. Maybe we're most like Christ when we're in a lonely place seeking renewal. "At daybreak Jesus went out to a solitary place. The people were looking for him and when they came to where he was, they tried to keep him from leaving them" (Luke 4:42).

There always will be needs and people pressing on us for our attention, but it's imperative that we seek to refresh our souls so we minister out of fullness, not out of emptiness. One of the saddest sights I've seen is the hollow, blank eyes of a burned out youth worker who has lost passion due to a lack of personal renewal.

The privilege of ministry is growth. To be effective, we need to make sure we're modeling for our students and leaders a person who is growing because he or she is being renewed—physically, emotionally, and spiritually. Our youth deserve to see a youth worker with a well-nurtured soul.

Endnotes

1. Marie Winn, *Children Without Childhood* (New York: Pantheon Books, 1993), 125.

2. Winn, *Children Without Childhood,* 134.

3. Stephen R. Covey, *The Seven Habits of Highly Effective People* (New York: Simon & Schuster, Inc., 1989), 32.

4. Stephen R. Covey, *Principle-Centered Leadership* (New York: Simon & Schuster, Inc., 1992), 37.

GROUP DISCUSSION QUESTIONS
Chapter 1: *A Passion for Souls*

1. Do you agree that powerful youth work requires a passion for kids—an intense desire for influence? Why or why not?

2. What disturbs you most about our culture in crisis? Why?

3. Why is it so easy to get caught up in the "numbers game"?

4. How does a youth worker balance his or her focus between the past, the present, and the future?

5. Synergy is what happens when teamwork reaches the next level so that the whole is more than the sum of the parts. Describe a time when you observed synergy.

6. Do you agree or disagree with the statement, "Youth work is more passion than profession?" Why?

Nurture Requires Change

*Nurture Your Soul With a
Commitment to Lifelong Learning*

I t was the era of long hair, Birkenstock sandals, and tie-dye T-shirts. Being a youth worker meant teaching teenagers "radical discipleship." It meant backpacking with the youth group and having heavy rap sessions (the kind you talk at, not dance to). It was the time for individuals to pursue their "own journey." People had their "own thing" to "get into." The youth in the church didn't trust the "establishment old-folks." The old folks hoped the youth director they hired would "teach these kids to respect their elders." In some regions, there was strong nationalism: "USA—Love it or leave it." Others struggled with a war that made little sense and a growing mistrust in government and leadership in general.

In the seventies we learned to "hang loose" and "let it be." It was a time of mixed messages. On one hand, we tried to be cool; on the other hand, we were really mad. The key word within the church became "renewal." The focus became revolutionizing structures that were old and ineffective.

Mod Squad

Those days, my hair was in a big puffy Afro, I wore shorts and sandals, and in my backpack I carried a book, *The Problem of Wineskins: Church Structure in a Technological Age* by Howard A. Snyder. It called for radical change. Snyder believed the church must be structured so it could affirm the uniqueness and value of human personality. It must insist that what is true of individuals is equally true of the church: It has value because it's a work of God.[1]

Snyder called for a new look at the church and affirmation of the value of the individual. The individual seemed at risk in the seventies. Technology was "crouching at the door," waiting to clone us all into "Stepford Wives." Snyder warned, "The church today lives in a world increasingly hostile to all that is human."[2]

If you worked with youth in the seventies, you might remember the Sunday school lessons you taught, fellowship on Sunday nights, the Wednesday night youth groups, the "fifth quarters" after football games—and how about those lock-ins? You enjoyed seeing the teenagers in the youth group three or four times a week. When you had sign-ups for camps, you always had to make a waiting list.

Times have changed, haven't they? Those of you who weren't involved in youth ministry in the seventies probably can't relate to this seemingly fictional narrative. There has been so much change, and it's almost impossible to relate to the seventies. Yet many of us still minister the way we did then. How about you? Do you still minister the way you did in the seventies? In the eighties? In the nineties?

Have you grown in the last decade? Or are you still doing what you have always done? The world is in flux. Are you growing with the changes and demands?

If we're to be effective and relevant youth workers, we need to learn to think trends, not tradition. We also need to evaluate our existing ministries to see if they reflect an awareness of the changes of our world. A seventies model won't cut it in the new millennium.

Consider these contrasts.

The Way It Was (Seventies)	The Way It's Going
Long hair	Short or shaved hair
3 TV networks	180 cable choices
Verbal orientation	Visual orientation
Office	Home office
Personal freedom	Control over environment
Desire for information	Desire for simplicity
FM radio	MTV and CD's
Loyalty/commitment	Options/choices
Most important resource—money	Most important resource—time
General service	Specialized service
Full service	Nichemanship
Data-driven decisions	Need-driven decisions
Change seen as optional	Change seen as mandatory
Focus on the individual	Focus on the group/family systems
Self-help	Network
Denial regarding dysfunction	Awareness of dysfunction
Intellectual solutions	Emotional resolutions
Decline in religion	Increase in spirituality
Outer structure reform	Inner recovery
Values—issues and altruism	Values—tangible benefit
Reform of existing structure	Entrepreneurial new structures
Top-down leadership	Bottom-up leadership
Outside-in perspective	Inside-out perspective
Pastor-centered leadership	Team-centered leadership
Male-dominated leadership	Women and men in leadership

Church as program	Church as relationships
Teaching center	Resource center
Casual, hang-loose style	Authenticity, consistency
Guru: John Lennon	Guru: John Gray
Taboo: stale thinking	Taboo: political incorrectness
What's in: experimentation	What's in: recovery

Learning From the Contrasts

Understanding the changes from decade to decade will help the perceptive youth worker know how to minister effectively. Ministry is finding a need and meeting it. Being aware of trends in our culture will enable us to be relevant to the youth we serve. It's been my experience that the church tends to change and adapt to the needs of society five to ten years after the shift in our culture. If we're to be relevant, we need to be current with cultural shifts and trends. We need to be on the growing edge.

Relevancy has a qualitative aspect to it as well. We need to be offering a youth ministry of substance and excellence. George Barna, in his discussion of effective churches, notes, "Undeniably, working with teenagers these days is a fascinating experience. The leaders at the growing churches concurred that ministering to children and youth today is even more demanding than in the past. Raised in a society in which cutthroat competition is commonplace, they are exposed to excellence in the quality of products and services, and they have come to expect excellence from the church, too. Today's young people are quality driven. They are not willing to accept mediocrity or to put up with ministry that is in a maintenance mode." [3]

We used to be able to get by with strumming a few chords on the guitar and singing "Pass It On." Now teenagers expect a praise band, complete with synthesizer, electronic drums, worship leaders, choreography, and lyrics projected on a huge screen. At youth groups in the seventies, we were casual, kicked back, and unconcerned with excellence. In fact, sloppiness was in. In 1975, I taught a six-month series on Acts in a black-widow-spider-infested "youth shack," and the teenagers packed it out!

Teenagers are much more sophisticated now. They aren't necessarily more mature, just more selective—they're used to having many options. A youth ministry that says, "Here we are! This is what we offer—fit into our programs" is destined to fail. If we're to be lifelong learners, we need to be students of the teenagers in our own youth groups. To do compelling youth ministry, we must be sensitive to three things.

• Be sensitive to students' different **levels of maturity.** Not all students are interested in what you may be offering. Your "fellowship" program might be perceived as "only for those without a social life." Your Bible study could be too challenging for some and boring to others.

We need to assess our students' various levels of maturity and interest and ask ourselves, "What do we have that meets them at this level and challenges them toward the next level of maturity?"

• Be sensitive to your students' **time restrictions.** It used to be that students would come to youth events three or four times in one week. Now time is students' most important resource. We need to assess our expectations regarding students' time.

Several years ago, we realized that our youth group wasn't making the kind of impact we wanted to make in our community, so we began asking ourselves questions.

• What are our attendance patterns?

• What kind of student is coming to each ministry?

• What are we providing to minister to different levels of maturity/interest?

• How have we demonstrated a sensitivity to the students' time restrictions?

As we considered these questions with our student leaders and adult staff, we made some illuminating discoveries. Our weekly schedule included a Tuesday night Campus Connection outreach and a Sunday evening Power Surge, which was designed to be a growth-level event that challenged Christian students to apply biblical principles to their lives. We were puzzled by the fact that students generally drifted toward one or the other weekly event rather than attending both. We were also perplexed by the difficulty we found recruiting staff for the Tuesday outreach, which was a high-energy night with innovative recreation, multimedia, music, drama, and short "safe" talks on hot topics.

I believe the program had not become weaker but had gotten out of step with the students. Losing sight of the cultural trends had caused us to be unrealistic in our expectations. We expected students to come on their own to Saturday or Sunday celebrations (our corporate worship times), attend Sunday night Bible study, and then invite their friends to a campus-oriented outreach on Tuesday night. On top of this weekly schedule, we offered monthly weekend events and camps. For us, in our culture, this was too much. It created subtle pressure on the students to be involved at a level that most weren't able to maintain. It created an unnecessary gulf separating the adult ministry teams that led different aspects of the program. We were feeling guilty because we weren't able to generate enough energy to draw students for a weekly outreach event. It also had made some student leaders feel they were "being used." One sixteen-year-old leader said, "You use us to get our friends here and to help with the little things, but you really don't trust us with the big decisions of our group." This comment jarred us into remembering what our students wanted:

- to be involved,
- to have choices,
- to work on a team,
- to have their needs met (not simply run a program),
- to know others authentically,
- to be proud of their group, and
- to enjoy genuine community.

As a result, we developed a Sunday morning program for students—churched and unchurched. It's a fun, upbeat environment that makes it easy for young people to invite friends. We no longer expect students to go to the "big church" celebration, which is clearly geared for adults. Instead, we have two youth services, one for middle school and one for high school. Each one has its own culture. We have students involved in planning, leading worship, playing instruments, doing skits, and leading games and table discussions. As a result, our attendance has grown significantly.

- Be sensitive to your students' desire for **something meaningful.**

For youth ministry to be worth students' time, we need a renewed commitment to activities that are inherently meaningful, then we need to make them fun. For decades, we have hosted fun events and have sought to infuse meaning into them. Many times I've felt like Jon Lovett's Pathological Liar when, after an hour of crowdbreakers and games, I segued with, "The point of the pie toss and pig wrestling was to show us the messiness of sin. Yeah, that's it!"

Sometimes we really stretch to reach meaningfulness. Students are looking for things to do which are meaningful *and* fun. Making fun the top priority usually means running out of resources (time, money, ideas, people, or energy) before we make it meaningful.

Effective ministry now means being the right person more than developing the right program. Students are bored with programs; they're too busy for hype. They want events to be fun, certainly, but the events must also be meaningful.

To be relevant to our students, we may need to make changes in ministry. Start with these three ideas in mind:
- Be sensitive to your students' differing levels of maturity.
- Be sensitive to your students' time restrictions.
- Be sensitive to your students' desire for something meaningful.

Seasons of a Ministry

Ministries go through seasons. What works in the "fall" of a ministry may die in the "winter." The wise youth worker is sensitive to the seasons of a ministry and is courageous enough to make the necessary adjustments.

In your ministry the adjustment might mean being willing to do less in order to do a better job at what you do. Nichemanship is the idea of focusing on what you do well and pouring your resources into that. It has a lot to do with giftedness. Having a full-service youth ministry with multiple programs, large budgets, and several staff teams is unrealistic for most of us. Simplicity and excellence will become marks of effective youth ministries. A number of valid ministries have gone to a simpler, gentler, kinder youth program so they can be more flexible, personal, meaningful, and relational.

Learning to Risk Change

Youth ministry used to look at change as optional, and major program changes were considered risky. But the trends we face in our culture make change mandatory. The real risk is traditional thinking that prevents staying relevant to the needs of our youth. Like the leaves that drop from the trees in the fall, some elements of your ministry may need to be dropped from season to season.

Nurture requires growth. Growth means change. As the gardener prunes a branch in early spring so the tree will bear more blossoms later in the season, you may need to prune a branch off your youth ministry to produce more fruit. Successful ministry in this era isn't bigger, it's simpler and more effective. Instead of building a Rolls Royce with all the amenities, we need to build a Jeep that is simple, rugged, durable, and flexible. Your most effective ministry planning tool may be your eraser.

George Barna discovered there were some things growing churches held in common: Church growth can be described as taking off of the body of Christ all outmoded or ineffective garments and clothing it instead with garments that identify it as the representative of Christ in this world. "Growing congregations consciously rejected common conventions in favor of developing a more comfortable or more meaningful approach to a specific aspect of ministry. They did not dismiss the importance of that aspect of outreach. Instead, they believed the same ministry could better be accomplished through a different approach."[4]

To experience the renewing work of the Holy Spirit in our ministries, we need to be willing to try new "wineskins"—new methodologies, structures, and approaches. By studying the trends of the day, we can effectively present the changeless message of the gospel to the people who need it most, in a way they can understand.

Learning to Be Teachable

Approaching life as a learner creates the perspective necessary for growth—and growth is the privilege of youth ministry. If we're teachable, we interpret all of life's situations and experiences as opportunities for learning and personal involvement.

This perspective liberates us to view failure as an opportunity to learn. Youth work isn't an exact science; a lot of what we do is a result of trial and error. We think a pizza night with Christian videos would be a great idea, so we try it, only to find out that on Friday nights most of the teenagers are working or out on dates. Be willing to try—even when we fail, the risk is worth it if we're willing to learn all we can from it.

Some of the failures I experienced in the early years of youth work were my greatest teachers.

Six Mistakes I Made in the Early Years

Mistake 1: Judging my value by the size of my youth group

In the early days of my youth ministry, having a youth group of only seven teenagers made me feel that I wasn't a valuable youth worker. I would easily get all seven in the church van and sheepishly drive to an event where some youth workers had two or three bus loads of teenagers. I felt small, insignificant, and embarrassed.

"What kind of youth worker are you?" I asked myself. As I thought about it, I realized I was relational, I could make people laugh, I was practical and athletic, and I liked to teach the Bible. I decided to focus these five characteristics on my seven teenagers. I learned that small is good because it's intimate, personal, and more caring, and it often means more impact than larger groups. And small is great in case you really fail—fewer people know!

Mistake 2: Judging my impact by the response of the teenagers

I had prepared what I thought was going to be a life-changing lesson for my magnificent seven. I had studied the Scriptures well and had memorized my lesson plan. I had developed creative learning activities and enthusiasm-inducing crowdbreakers. I even had brought refreshments! The whole night was set up for significant life change. There was only one problem—nobody came! I waited fifteen minutes and began calling. I called the *entire* youth group and only got hold of Chris, who said she'd be right over. Chris showed up, and we ate cookies and drank red church punch while I explained all the fun stuff I had planned.

She looked at me compassionately and said, "I'm sorry no one else came. It looks like it would have been great, but can we talk about something that's bothering me?"

We had a very frank two-hour conversation about some serious personal issues in her life. Ten years later, reflecting on our old group, she said, "I'll never forget that night you dumped all your plans and helped me with my problems. I knew then that I was more important than your program."

People are more important than programs. It took the failure of a program to help me learn to evaluate my impact based on relationships, not the success of my program.

Mistake 3: Thinking I could do it alone

There was a time I tried to fix the van, drive the van, plan the games, lead the games, cook the meals, teach the lesson, and counsel the students. After a few retreats flying solo, I decided I needed to get help or quit youth work. I was young and energetic, so I had thought I could do it all. I realized I couldn't do it all and that I was robbing others of the joy of participation and service.

Once I decided to involve others, I discovered they had been there all along. What had kept them from surfacing? My attitude. When we're young and insecure, we're tempted to build the youth group around us. Many young youth workers fall into the Pied Piper syndrome. They like to solo on their float and have a parade of young people follow them. The Pied Piper works for fairy tales and parades, but it's a lousy model for youth ministry.

Another reason we find ourselves alone in youth work is that we're afraid. We may be afraid of losing control or afraid of other adults. Some youth workers are comfortable with youth but not with other adults. This doesn't mean they're good youth workers—it means they haven't learned to relate to other adults. In fact, their inability to relate well to other adults hinders their impact on teenagers because they don't provide a positive model of adult-to-adult relationships.

I discovered help was available for the asking. For example, there was Mr. Botham, a retired mechanic who came from Sweden where he worked on great ships and ocean liners.

"Mr. Botham, would you be willing to be the mechanic for the church van? I don't have the time or the skills." I sheepishly asked.

"Shoor, shoor sonny. Dat would be no problem," replied Mr. Botham. For years he kept that old van in running condition. I was relieved, and so were the church board and the parents.

Sue attended college out of town but came home every weekend. She considered helping on our youth staff but didn't think she had anything to offer. "I'm shy, and I don't know the Bible that well. I like the teenagers, but I don't know how I can help."

"What do you like to do?" I asked.

"I like to ride horses, cook, and organize things."

"How would you like to help me with the food for our retreats and events?"

I asked (with a sense of urgency).

"I'd love to do it!"

I was relieved, affirmed, and excited all at once. Relieved because I hate buying food, organizing it, and cooking it. Sue loved to do this; she even *enjoyed* washing dishes and cleaning up! I felt affirmed because the Spirit of God was calling people to be a part of our ministry by using their strengths and gifts. I also felt excited because I began to understand that I didn't have to do it all. In fact, others were excited about helping me!

Later Sue organized regular horseback-riding Bible studies. A group would ride to a lake, study the Bible together, swim, and ride back. Sue was working in her area of giftedness, and God blessed it!

Thinking I could do it alone led to failure, but it also led to an influential lesson: "Learn to lead with your strength and staff to your weakness." I had made the pleasant discovery that I could minister with the things I did well and look for people to complement my weakness.

Mistake 4: Not trusting anyone over thirty

When I began youth work in the early seventies, there was an atmosphere of suspicion between my generation and the "old fogies." I contributed to this alienation by avoiding interaction with parents, keeping the youth group out of the mainstream of church life, and not recruiting staff more than twenty-five years old.

My suspicion and distrust kept me and my youth group from growing. A lack of trust guarantees stagnation. Later, I learned that parents aren't the enemy, that the youth and the rest of the church benefit by interaction, and that staff over twenty-five have much to offer. I learned that parents are far more committed to their children's growth and well-being than I was as the youth pastor. I learned that youth enjoyed being with the adults in the church at a properly designed event. I discovered that my most faithful and effective youth workers weren't the cool college types, but those who were older. In fact, some of the most effective staff people have been parents or grandparents who already have raised their children. Not trusting anyone over thirty was *my* problem—the "problem" had nothing to do with the individuals who had lived longer than I had.

Mistake 5: Being relational with no goal in mind

In my early days of youth work, I wanted to show the teenagers that I was cool, that I understood them, and that I could relate. I wanted to show them that I was one of them. This was easy to do because I was ministering as a part-time youth director and was only two years older than two of the seven teenagers in my group. I had picked up from Young Life the motto, "Earn the right to be heard," and I took it to the extreme. "Earning the right to be heard" wasn't supposed to mean taking a year to mention God or personal spiritual issues.

I learned from this mistake that I was operating out of a fear of rejection. "If I try to deal with serious issues, they might not come to the group," I thought. Or worse, "They might reject *me!*" I reasoned. Hanging out but not moving forward in relationships isn't healthy for the youth worker or the students. I realize that now, but it took an angry senior named Steve to help me see my failure.

"How come you never correct us or offer us guidance? I could really use some direction, or someone to kick me in the tail and say 'get going!'" he admonished.

As I thought about my passiveness, I realized that I was timid and that timidity was not a quality of spiritual leadership. Steve's admonition, along with God's Word, helped me learn that we need to be both relational and intentional.

"For God did not give us a spirit of timidity, but a spirit of power, of love and of self-discipline" (2 Timothy 1:7).

Mistake 6: Not challenging students to serve or lead

Because I was more concerned with being liked than being a leader, I seldom challenged my students to serve or lead. I challenged them to study the Bible, to pray, and to attend youth group, but I hadn't yet learned the value of praxis—the art of practicing what you have learned. I taught a lesson on servanthood but didn't offer the teenagers an opportunity to serve. I encouraged them to study the Bible but never held them accountable for what they studied. When I think of it, I may have done more harm than good in terms of their spiritual journey. They learned from me—their youth pastor—that Christianity is something you know, not something you do.

I was quick to respond to their felt needs ("Let's go water-skiing!"), and at college I was learning about the needs young people are *supposed* to have, but I hadn't become aware of their real needs.

Robert was the intellectual in the group. He helped me discover that I wasn't challenging the group. "How long do you think it takes before we're ready to do something about what you've been teaching?" he asked.

"A little longer?" I sheepishly responded.

"I was ready six months ago. It's not that complex. If all we do is sit in here and talk about it, we'll never really learn it. Kids need to do stuff if they're really gonna learn it."

I sensed some impatience in his voice. I knew he was brighter than the average bear, and I also knew he was right. It was time to move on. It was time to challenge the troops to move out. I called the whole group together for our first leadership meeting. Six out of seven showed up.

"These six will lead the other one," I reasoned.

At that meeting I said, "For too long now, I've been doing the talking and you've been doing the listening. It has been suggested that we now start to let you talk more and do more. What do you think?"

My new leadership team responded with enthusiasm; they decided we needed to have more discussion and less lecture from me. They picked one student to help lead the discussions by having him lead a small group (three to five people!) They each decided what they could do.

• Steve would clean up the youth room and get some kids to help paint it.

• Chris would be the liaison between her Campus Life club and our youth group to give us access to all the events they were offering.

• Robert would research options for service projects.

• Robanne would see if she could get her dad to donate some furniture from his store for the youth room.

• Rochelle would ask her mom if we could have weekly meetings at her home (they had the nicest pool!).

• Roger would ask his dad about getting free tickets to a baseball game for the whole group and friends we'd invite.

I sat there dumbfounded. There was more energy and motivation in that room during that one meeting than there had been in the previous six months of youth work. The teenagers were fired up and ready to go. I realized then that I had failed to understand that most teenagers want to be challenged to lead or serve. All we need to do is offer them choices.

Out of that first meeting, we acquired a redecorated and furnished youth room. We went to monthly events planned by Campus Life (riding in our faithful van). We began simple service projects, such as visiting convalescent homes and taking food and clothing to Mexico. Parents began to offer their homes, pools, food, RVs, and cabins for the youth group's use (all we had to do was have a student ask), and we went to a bunch of Padres games (thanks, Roger!).

Steve, the guy who was "volunteered" to help lead the discussion group, liked it so much he continued it in college. He did such a good job with youth that I delegated the junior high group to him, and he led it with a passion. To date, he has served more than twenty years as a youth pastor.

The privilege of youth work is the fruit. I'm grateful to have "stumbled" on the need to challenge teenagers to serve and lead. It brings me great joy.

"I thank my God every time I remember you. In all my prayers for all of you, I always pray with joy because of your partnership in the gospel from the first day until now, being confident of this, that he who began a good work in you will carry it on to completion until the day of Christ Jesus" (Philippians 1:3-6).

We have a window of opportunity to become relevant to the youth of our culture. The older they get, the less likely they are to consider the claims of Christ. The time to act is now. All growth involves change, and all change is risky. "There is a time for everything and a season for every activity under heaven…a time to plant and a time to uproot…a time to keep and a time to throw away" (Ecclesiastes 3).

We live in an age of cataclysmic change. Instead of denying it, we need to seize the day and see change as an opportunity rather than an opponent. Young people are searching for what most youth groups are offering. We need to build bridges into their world so they can find it. Change is an inevitable part of nurture.

The bond we share today with the people of the last millennial era is the sense of living in a time of enormous change. The last time the United States experienced such a deeply religious period was during the nineteenth century, when the country's economy changed from agricultural to industrial. When people are buffeted by change, the need for spiritual belief intensifies. [5]

Endnotes

1. Howard A. Snyder, *The Problem of Wineskins* (Downers Grove, IL: InterVarsity Press, 1975), 122.

2. Snyder, *The Problem of Wineskins,* 113.

3. George Barna, *User Friendly Churches* (Ventura, CA: Regal Books, 1991) 125.

4. Barna, *User Friendly Churches,* 172-173.

5. John and Aburdene Naisbitt, *Megatrends 2000: Ten New Directions for the 1990's* (New York: William Morrow and Company, Inc., 1990), 271-272.

GROUP DISCUSSION QUESTIONS
Chapter 2: *Nurture Requires Change*

Nurture Your Soul With a Commitment to Lifelong Learning

1. Discuss the contrasts between "The Way It Was (Seventies)" and "The Way It's Going" (p. 23).

2. How do these changes create the potential for more effective youth work in the future?

3. George Barna states, "Today's young people are quality driven." How have you experienced this in your youth work?

4. Do you think most students are looking for something more meaningful from a youth group? Why or why not?

5. Which of the six mistakes I made in the early years (pp. 29-32) do you most closely identify with? Why?

6. Considering the trends of today, how can you become more relevant to youth in your area?

CHAPTER 3
The Way Up Is Down

Nurture Your Soul by Serving

"That's a nice fluffy bun!" I thought as I bit into my seventeenth Big Mac of the month. I am amazed at the consistency of quality McDonald's maintains across the country and throughout the world. As I sat there in my yellow plastic chair, doing research on quality service, it occurred to me that McDonald's really demonstrates excellence through

- consistency,
- cleanliness,
- friendly service,
- quick response, and
- value.

As I thought about these qualities, I realized that they are also hallmarks of an effective youth ministry. McDonald's knows these specific aspects of excellence are crucial if it is to be effective in hamburger sales. McDonald's knows its customers. The organization understands that customers want to be able to go into any McDonald's restaurant and find the qualities they expect. Consistency helps build customer confidence and customer loyalty. If customers are loyal, they'll return for repeat business. Selling one hamburger isn't as important as gaining a repeat customer.

McDonald's also knows that cleanliness makes its restaurants distinctive. McDonald's introduced an industry standard for cleanliness that was quickly adopted by other fast-food franchises. You can count on McDonald's restaurants to be clean and friendly. If you step up to the counter to order, you'll be greeted by a neat, smiling, uniformed employee who cheerfully says, "Welcome to McDonald's. May I take your order, please?"

McDonald's isn't just friendly. It's user-friendly. You can spot the golden arches from a hundred yards away, even if you're going fifty-five miles per hour on the freeway. When you walk into the store, you feel comfortable because it looks familiar: The floor plan, decorations, menu, and uniforms all look like the McDonald's back home. You haven't been greeted yet, but you feel welcome. When your kids see the play equipment, you become a hero for taking them to a fun place to eat.

If you're in a hurry, McDonald's responds to your need in record time. You can zip through the drive-through and be on your way faster than you can get a snack at home during a commercial. McDonald's restaurants don't offer everything, but you can count on getting what they do offer quickly and with remarkable quality. They have defined their niche and developed excellence.

Value is one of the distinctives of McDonald's. You can buy a tasty burger for the price of a side order at a coffee shop. People eat at McDonald's because they can afford to and they get good food. It may not be gourmet, but at least the kids like it. In five minutes you can have a spread laid out for you and the kids, and it costs just a little more than cooking at home—plus there's no cleanup or dirty dishes!

Ministry should be like McDonald's—consistent, distinctive, user-friendly, responsive, and offering value. We should be close to the customer—real close.

A simple message permeates the atmosphere. All business success rests on something labeled a sale, which at least momentarily weds company and customer. The excellent companies *really are* close to their customers. That's it. Other companies talk about it; the excellent companies do it. [1]

Ministry is meeting needs. To meet people's needs, we have to be close enough to know what those needs are and how to meet them. The Bible tells us that a good shepherd knows his sheep (John 10:14). He knows their peculiarities and particular needs. He can tell by the slight limp of a lamb that she might have stepped on a burr. He can glance at the flock and know who is missing. He knows which ewe is pregnant and in need of extra food and water. He also is alert to the one sheep who is characteristically late and often left behind because he is a straggler. A good shepherd knows his sheep, and they know his voice. Being close means not only knowing our sheep but letting them know us. Effective youth workers are service-oriented because they're sensitive to needs, user-friendly, and responsive.

Youth workers can learn something from well-run restaurants such as McDonald's. We learn about service and teamwork from the late Ray Kroc, the founder of McDonald's and former owner of the San Diego Padres.

A well-run restaurant is like a winning baseball team. It makes the most of every crew member's talent and takes advantage of every split-second opportunity to speed up service. [2]

You may not think of yourself as being in the service business, but you are. Youth workers are in a service business of offering grace and truth to young people. It's our aspiration to make the most of every teenager's potential. We don't have much time with teenagers, so we need to be quick to respond. We have limited opportunities to impact the teenagers God has entrusted to us. To maximize these opportunities, effective youth workers have discovered the secret of being a servant and empowering youth through giving them opportunities to serve.

Four Ways to Empower Through Serving

1. Influential youth workers know how to build **significance** into serving. They create a vision that allows teenagers to see themselves at the center of something meaningful and necessary.

    Joey was a timid and withdrawn teenager in our youth group. He came occasionally, but not enough for us to really get to know him.

One day I gave him a ride home and asked, "What do you like to do?"

"Ah, not much. I like playing battle games at the park at night. But not too much else," replied Joey.

"Would you like to go to Mexico on a mission and help me with the games? I could use someone to keep the kids busy in the afternoons—you know, soccer and volleyball?" I asked.

"Sure, I'll do that." Joey promised.

I was surprised he agreed that easily, but he went. When we crossed the border, Joey changed—he went from shy, withdrawn, and passive to outgoing, loud, and active. He was on a mission. He spent each day in the village actively playing with the kids for six or eight hours. When we'd return to our campsite, he'd collapse, totally exhausted. Mexico changed Joey because it made him feel significant; it gave him an opportunity to serve, and his contributions were valued. The children in the village loved Joey because he would play with them, wrestle with them, and tickle them. Many of these children never had felt this kind of attention and affection from a man, and, even though Joey was only fifteen, he met a need in the lives of these children.

I asked Joey why Mexico meant so much to him.

"In Mexico I feel important because I can give something those kids need—attention. My parents are divorced, and I never got any attention from my dad. I know how much kids need it. Playing with those kids is my mission, I just gotta do it."

Mexico was so important to Joey that he has gone back six times. We empower our teenagers when we give them opportunities to gain significance through serving.

2. Effective youth workers understand the importance of **competence** and are committed to developing it in themselves and their teenagers. Competence is a key element of empowerment. This doesn't mean perfection, but a commitment to growth and learning on the job. Empowered youth workers can look at a failure and ask, "What can we learn from this?" Working to become competent involves risk and the possibility of failure, but always in the environment of developing.

People reach high standards of performance when they have a sense of mastery over lower standards and feel successful enough to reach for the more challenging standards. I helped Joey plan the games that would be appropriate for the Mexican children. I had been there and knew what would work. Joey was responsible for obtaining the recreation equipment and recruiting volunteers. This was a challenge for him the first year, but he was competent. The second trip, he initiated higher standards for recreation and needed very little help from me. Joey felt competent, and it empowered him and our Mexico mission to achieve new levels of effectiveness.

3. Youth workers who impact lives understand the value of **community.** Community is a sense of reliance on one another toward a common cause. If the common cause is service, an environment of significance, competence, and community will develop. Many youth groups fail to develop community because they don't have a compelling cause. Being together to be together is not enough, but going to Mexico to love the children and tell them of Jesus' love is a compelling cause.

Erin was having a difficult time breaking into our youth group. She said the group was "cliquish and not interested in me." Then she took a risk, joined our choir and drama group, and went on tour.

"I'll give this group one last chance to see if I can feel accepted. If it doesn't happen on this tour, I'm going to another church," she said. The choir and drama group traveled from town to town, singing and performing for hundreds of people. At one small town, she and a friend were asked to sing for a dying woman in the hospital. Erin went, and halfway through the song she was overwhelmed by the dying woman's tears of appreciation. She realized she was offering words of grace and truth to this woman. They were words of hope and significance. God was using her! Her focus shifted from potential rejection to being a significant part of a team. Needless to say, Erin discovered the value of community.

4. Highly capable youth workers have discovered that **fun** is a key ingredient of empowerment. Fun creates energy. Some of the most festive times I've had have come in the midst of challenging circumstances.

After a day of draining ministry in the deserts of Mexicali, Mexico, our ministry team was starving, thirsty, and not interested in going back to the camp for cafeteria-type food. I pulled the bus into my favorite taco stand and announced, "We're going to ditch the evening meeting at camp, skip dinner, and eat here. I want everyone to try a taco. I'll buy the first round!" I spent fifty dollars that night on tacos, but the experience was worth every penny. We sat there for hours, laughing, drinking gallons of Pepsi, and seeing how hot we could handle our salsa. We had been warned by the camp leaders not to eat in these stands, but I knew Lupe made the best tacos in the valley, and I asked God to heal the tacos so we wouldn't get sick.

The teenagers enjoyed the comfort of the restaurant after eating outside for days. The relaxation and the stories seemed to recharge our spirits. That night at the taco stand, we discovered many funny and interesting things that had happened that we wouldn't have had time to hear about if we had gone back to camp for the usual late-night meeting. Building community requires time for community laughter. It usually helps to have food around, too. Feeling empowered to serve grows out of an environment of enjoyment. Service doesn't have to be a burden we endure; it can be an opportunity that inspires us.

Youth work is more than just meeting needs. It's also enjoying each other and sharing fun times together. Teenagers will feel significant if we begin with activities that are meaningful and make them fun. Almost any project or experience can be made fun. You have to look for it—kind of like finding a taco stand, at night, in the middle of the Mexican desert.

Being Environmentally Aware

Faithful servants are aware of their surroundings. They know what the available resources are and even anticipate the needs of the people they're serving. They're alert to their environment. To be effective in youth ministry we need to be aware of the environment. We need to realize that teenagers are at different levels of spiritual interest. One program can't meet the needs of all the teenagers you hope to reach.

At our church, we target the different levels of spiritual maturity in students. One of the most helpful illustrations of these different levels can be found in Doug Fields' excellent book, *Purpose-Driven Youth Ministry*. Doug shows five levels of spiritual maturity in concentric circles to suggest a ministry target:[3]

In youth ministry we have potential audiences with different levels of spiritual maturity:
  • the non-Christian student (community)
  • the new Christian (crowd)

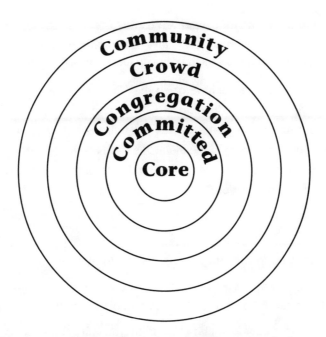

- the stagnant Christian who isn't growing (congregation)
- the growing Christian student (committed)
- the mature spiritual leader (core)

The growing Christian student (committed) may be your favorite level, and you may want to ignore the other four. But they won't go away. Every teenage population has at least five levels of spiritual maturity we need to address. If we don't address them, we'll have a smaller group and a less mature group. Even if we focus only on working with the growing Christian students, they'll miss out on the growth opportunities they would have by reaching out to non-Christian students. In other words, the "committed" and the "core" need the "crowd" and the "community" to grow.

Circles of Commitment [4]

Those in the outside circle, the *community* students, are the ones who live within the area, probably within a reasonable driving distance of your church. They are not the Christian students, but the unchurched young people in middle school and high school.

The *crowd* students are represented by the next circle. They're the students who come with the crowd and "check things out." They may fill out a card or pick up a flyer for an event. They may even come to several activities. Their commitment is expressed in being there, usually nothing more. Some are regular attendees, but they haven't been changed by the gospel message.

Congregation students have given their lives to Christ. They belong to the body of Christ and need fellowship. In our ministry, we encourage these students to get involved in small groups because we believe they need the small groups to grow. Young people need the friendships and the accountability they find in small groups. We have two sayings that remind us of the need for youth to be in a small-group congregation:

"Students grow in community." They grow better when they grow with friends.

"People only do what they're *inspected* to do." People need accountability.

Committed students are the ones who are willing to spend time developing spiritual disciplines. Sometimes we call them disciples. These are the teenagers who have a hunger for God's Word and spend time studying and memorizing it. They have a zeal to pray and enjoy worship. Some of our most meaningful times are student-led worship times. We have students who meet every Thursday just to worship. The youth pastor or leader doesn't have to attend. The focus is on God. Now these students are committed!

Core students are the committed teenagers who have discovered their gifts and the joy of service. They have the opportunity to serve young people at the other levels (in the other circles). I've seen students move from "community" all the way to "core," and then begin to reach out to "community" youth. This is what youth ministry is all about!

Evaluate the ministries you're offering your students. If they're all community or crowd offerings, you're missing some teenagers. To ignore any one of these levels is to ignore students in your group.

Our aspiration is to build a ministry that is environmentally aware by ministering to teenagers at each of these levels. Notice that the higher the commitment, the fewer students are involved. The largest circle is the community circle which involves no investment. The congregation circle gets smaller; and smaller still are the committed and the core circles.

Jesus had the same experience. When he offered miracles and a free lunch, he had a crowd. When he asked them to follow him, the number dropped down to seventy-two. We know he spent much time with his faithful band of twelve, but when it came down to it, he was more intimate with two or three. The higher the commitment, the fewer people will follow. Still, Jesus was available to people at all levels of following.

Your perspective may keep you from ministering to one or more of these levels. It's important that you evaluate your assumptions about the people you serve. Here are some common assumptions.

- Teenagers need to be entertained.
- Teenagers don't want to be challenged.
- Our teenagers don't have non-Christian friends.
- Everyone in our group is a Christian.
- Teenagers would rather play than serve.

If these are your assumptions about youth ministry, they'll shape your programming. The way you see something and give order to it is called your paradigm. Paradigms give order and structure to our perceptions. *Paradigm* comes from the Greek word *paradeigma,* which means a pattern or map for understanding and explaining certain aspects of reality. It's how you look at the world. Your paradigm will define your ministry. If your paradigm includes the five listed assumptions, you won't feel any need to have events that are attractive to non-Christian teenagers; nor will you feel the need to develop committed- and core-level events to help your teenagers experience ministry opportunities and service. Chances are, you'll be working with a small group of Christian students who are in cliques and don't get along.

To be effective servants/youth workers, we need to examine our paradigms. To help you do this, consider the following questions:

- What has been successful in the past? Are we slaves to it?

- How has our teenage population changed? Have we adapted to it?

- What needs now exist that didn't exist a few years ago? What can we do about them?

- What area would yield the greatest results if we gave it a little more attention?

- What's impossible to do today but would fundamentally change our youth ministry if we could do it?

These questions will help you "draw outside the lines."

One of my favorite TV commercials is the Isuzu Rodeo commercial where the teacher says, "Color inside the lines, the lines are our friends. Stay inside the lines." The camera pans to a woman driving a Rodeo. She smiles, and, with a look of abandon and excitement, she shifts into another paradigm as she careens off the road, "outside the lines," shifting into four-wheel drive for a blaze of off-road thrills.

We need to draw outside the lines if we want to see the world anew. We need a paradigm shift from what youth ministry was to what it can be. Someone once reminded me, "Your past success guarantees nothing." In fact, your successful past may block your vision of the future. Sometimes our pride gets in the way of what God wants to do in our youth ministry. That's why it's crucial to stay humble, stay flexible, stay open, and be responsive—to be a servant!

Ten Ways to Serve

1. Return all phone calls and e-mail within twenty-four hours.

2. Call or e-mail teenagers for no other reason than just to say "hello."

3. Inform parents completely of all details for events.

4. Take at least one teenager to lunch each week.

5. Do more listening than talking.

6. Go to student recitals or events that few people attend.

7. Spend time with youth volunteers.

8. Survey your teenagers' needs.

9. Form partnerships with the parents of your teenagers.

10. Set a weekly goal to serve a teenager at each level of your ministry.

Endnotes

1. Thomas Peters and Robert H. Waterman, Jr., *In Search of Excellence* (New York: Warner Books, 1982), 156.

2. Peters and Waterman, Jr., *In Search of Excellence,* 255.

3. Doug Fields, *Purpose-Driven Youth Ministry* (Grand Rapids, MI; Zondervan Publishing House, 1997), 87.

4. Adapted from Fields, *Purpose-Driven Youth Ministry,* 87-92.

GROUP DISCUSSION QUESTIONS
Chapter 3: *The Way Up Is Down*
Nurture Your Soul by Serving

1. Do you think McDonald's is a good model for youth ministry? Why or why not?

2. What can you, as a youth worker, do to be close to your "customer"?

3. Describe various youth activities that are designed to be environmentally aware—meeting needs of teenagers at different levels.

4. What do you think about the five assumptions that are discussed on page 45?

5. What need do our teenagers have that we could best meet if we gave it a little of our attention?

6. What's impossible to do today but would fundamentally change our youth ministry if we could do it?

7. Discuss the "Ten Ways to Serve" listed on page 46.

Power Surge

*Nurture Your Soul by Radiating the
Positive Power of the Holy Spirit*

I opened the refrigerator and stared at the chilled leftover lima beans—they were bleached pale green; they were wrinkled; and they had a bland smell. I popped one in my mouth but tasted nothing; I felt the fibrous texture, but the flavor was gone. It was an empty experience. Hoping for something nutritious and appetizing, I had encountered pale, tasteless, bland lima beans.

Then it hit me. I know some human leftover lima beans! Cold, pallid, bland, and boring, these people have become the frozen chosen! Instead of being alive and enthusiastic, they're lifeless and stagnant. They lead lives of quiet desperation—they're like soda that has lost its fizz.

Powerful youth workers have discovered the secret of enthusiasm. They know youth work can be extremely draining emotionally and physically. Still, you can be enthusiastic even if you aren't a twenty-two-year-old aerobics instructor. The secret of enthusiasm isn't physical; it's a spiritual principle. "For the kingdom of God is not a matter of eating and drinking, but of righteousness, peace and joy in the Holy Spirit" (Romans 14:17).

In youth ministry we don't simply build youth groups; we build the kingdom of God. The kingdom of God is where God rules in honor, glory, and majesty. Sometimes we get trapped in the methodology—the "eating and drinking" of youth work—and forget the spiritual element: the power of the Spirit. Enthusiastic youth workers have discovered how to radiate the positive power of the Holy Spirit.

The word "enthusiasm" comes from Greek words that mean "filled with God." To be genuinely enthusiastic means to be motivated, controlled, and influenced by God. It means that
- things that excite God excite you,
- God's values become your values,
- things that please God please you, and
- things that displease God displease you.

Enthusiasm is more than an external shell of quasi-inspiration and hype. It's an outward expression of something good on the inside. It looks good on the outside because it's right on the inside. Our enthusiasm is a mark of God's ownership—it shows that we belong to the risen Christ.

Several years ago our youth ministry staff was developing a list of the qualities we wanted to see in our student leaders. We decided we wanted our leaders to be F.A.T. Not fat, but F.A.T.—faithful, available, and teachable. We began to define and describe what we meant by each of these characteristics. However, after months of developing our student leader team, we still felt that something was missing.

We had faithful student leaders—they completed their tasks and were responsible. They were available and spent much of their time serving their peers. They also were teachable and dutifully took notes and maintained their ministry notebooks in a way that helped them learn and grow. But there was still something missing.

Then came the "aha" moment. As I talked with some adult leaders, I asked,

"What's missing from our student leaders? They're F.A.T., but it's not enough."

One youth worker replied, "There isn't the power or the excitement."

"Yeah, that's it!" offered another, "They need to use the Force." (*Star Wars* was big then.)

"Enthusiasm!" I exclaimed, "That's what we're missing. They're faithful, available, teachable, and *boring*! These kids need to discover the excitement of living on the edge that comes with the power of the Holy Spirit. We need to have 'fatty' leaders: F.A.T.E., with the E for enthusiasm! What good is it to have solid leaders if their lives don't reflect the power and the mystery of God?"

I began a study of enthusiasm, and I discovered that, to reach people for Christ, we need to understand and apply the principle of Spirit-driven enthusiasm. Can you think of a person who radiates the positive power of the Holy Spirit? What impact has that person had on your life? When I asked my staff these questions, I learned that every staff member had been profoundly influenced by someone who radiated the positive power of the Spirit.

"May the God of hope fill you with all joy and peace as you trust in him, so that you may overflow with hope by the power of the Holy Spirit" (Romans 15:13).

When a person is under the influence of the Holy Spirit, others will notice it. The early church was able to select leaders based on this observable quality. "Brothers, choose seven men from among you who are known to be full of the Spirit and wisdom" (Acts 6:3a).

When a person is under the direction of the Spirit, there will be supernatural results. These don't come from mere human effort or positive thinking; they're gifts of God's grace made evident in our own lives (Galatians 5:22-25).

We aren't supposed to let wine or anything else control us. We're to be under the influence of the Holy Spirit (Ephesians 5:18). When we're under the Spirit's control, we experience power, joy, and enthusiasm. Other people notice the effect (and so does God). "Anyone who serves Christ in this way is pleasing to God and approved by men" (Romans 14:18).

What a compliment—to be pleasing to God and approved by people! That's a desirable goal.

Today's teenagers are looking for joy, having already discovered that happiness is temporary. They're desperate for peace. They often encounter battles at home. In a world that can seem very gloomy, our young people are starving for hope; and they're looking for choices even as options seem to be declining. They long for a degree of power in their lives.

In this age our adolescents ache for hope, joy, peace, and power. And these are the qualities a youth worker empowered by the Spirit can effectively model.

One of the most attractive qualities in a person is joy. It's contagious. We want to be around people who exude joy. We want to know their secret. Joy comes from delighting in what God is doing. It's taking pleasure in what God has provided. It's seeing the little things as causes for celebration. It's taking time to see and exalt as eternity breaks into our temporal world. Genuine joy comes to those who have devoted themselves to something greater than personal happiness.

John Ortberg offers a practical suggestion to invite joy into our lives: "Devote a specific day to acts of celebration so that eventually joy will infuse your entire life. One day a week eat foods you love to eat, listen to music that moves your soul, play a sport that stretches and challenges you, read books that refresh your spirit, wear clothes that make you happy, surround yourself with beauty—and as you do these things, give thanks to God for his wonderful goodness. Reflect on what a gracious God he is to have thought of these gifts. Take the time to experience and savor joy, then direct your heart toward God so that you come to *know* he is the giver of '*every* good and perfect gift.' Nothing is too small if it produces true joy in us and causes us to turn toward God in gratitude and delight."[1]

When we display joy, we're reflecting God's basic character. We're demonstrating to a watching world that God is very serious about joy. God wants us to know joy because, when we know joy, we know God. God created us to reflect his joy. Jesus exuded a joy that was attractive to the crowds; they wanted to know its source.

This same joy is available to us. Jesus promised that we, too, can be filled with joy. "I have said these things to you so that *my* joy may be in you, and that your joy may be complete" (John 15:11, author's emphasis).

Then why aren't we joyful the way Jesus was?

I think our lack of joyfulness could be due to the joy-robbers in our culture. Our culture is very focused on the externals—on perceptions—but joy is something that grows from the inside out.

The Personality Myth

We live in a culture enchanted with externals. Popularity, possessions, and status are the standards by which we measure ourselves. This enchantment makes it difficult to remember how internally energizing the Holy Spirit can be. It seems so mystical, so subjective, even spooky. After all, we're talking about a spirit. Because we're bewitched by the externals, we find it very easy to emphasize personality rather than character.

In his study of success literature, Stephen R. Covey noticed that, shortly after World War I, the basic view of success shifted from the character ethic to what might be called the "Personality Ethic." "Success became more a function of personality, of public image, of attitudes and behaviors, skills and techniques, that lubricate the processes of human interaction. This Personality Ethic essentially took two paths: one was human and public relations techniques, and the other was positive mental attitude."[2]

In our culture, people are rewarded for personality more than character. In fact, being a person of character can bring punishment. Consider the "standard operating procedures" of some businesses, which bend the ethical line to maximize the profit margin. If you're a person of honesty, you may find yourself in conflict with the corporate culture, and you may lose financially, socially, or vocationally. There has been a shift in what our culture considers successful. In an era that barks, "Image is everything!" it's easy to get lost in all the hype and gloss.

Prior to World War I, personal character was considered a building block for success. The golden rule and qualities such as honesty, integrity, humility, courage, loyalty, justice, patience, industry, simplicity, and modesty were the hallmarks of effective living. A word that sounds archaic today is "temperance," which means "self-restraint in conduct, expression, indulgence of the appetites, etc.; moderation." This concept is so foreign in this age of excess that its meaning is almost forgotten. Yet, in days gone by, temperance was an admirable trait and was expected of a person with character. Now such a person would be dismissed as prudish or not politically correct.

The shift from character ethic to personality ethic has left a craving for image. Status, reputation, and position now determine worth. It's not *who* a person is, but *what* that person has. The personality myth teaches that the goal is to be liked, so do what it takes to be liked. This obsession with externals focuses on what people *do* rather than who those people *are*. It makes individuals vulnerable to the opinions of others, and often it compels people to strive to earn and achieve so they'll have the goods that will proclaim their worth. If our basis for self-worth is the personality ethic, we'll be very insecure because our security will be determined by the shifting perspective of others. The personality ethic is weak because it reinforces a fear of adversity, which may challenge the source of worth. Therefore, an individual may do anything to maintain the facade, so as not to risk being exposed as simply a player in the "age of flash."

The most tragic effect of the personality ethic is that it confuses the goals. The personality ethic says that the goal is to be liked. The character ethic says that the goal is to be like Christ. A youth worker who looks to the personality ethic for self-worth may be tempted to behave unethically or shrink from being effective in order to gain popularity. If the person's goal is to be like Christ, he or she will have a mental picture of what to do even if it isn't the most popular option.

The character ethic acknowledges that God develops character in the lives of people who are open to the reforming power of the Holy Spirit. This relationship with God is critical for character development. Oswald Chambers reminds us of this truth: "We must never allow anything to damage our relationship with God, but if something does damage it, we must take the time to make it right again. The most important aspect of Christianity is *not the work we do, but the relationship we maintain* and the surrounding influence and qualities produced by that relationship. That is all God asks us to give our attention to, and it is the one thing that is continually under attack."[3]

We have had a paradigm shift from principles to popularity, from absolutes to relative options, from character-based self-worth to personality-based self-worth—from character-based ethics to personality ethics. A youth worker who is influenced by the subjective ethical environment will believe that the most important aspect of Christianity is the work he or she accomplishes, not a growing and maturing relationship with God.

My team and I have contrasted the personality ethic with the character ethic. We've developed the following chart, which helps us see the implications of the character ethic for a principle-based ministry.

PERSONALITY ETHIC (Externally based)	VS.	CHARACTER ETHIC (Principle-based)	IMPLICATIONS FOR MINISTRY
Goal: to be liked		Goal: to be like Christ	I don't have to base ministry on people's reaction to me, but on whether I am helping others and myself become more like Christ.
Focus: What I Do		Focus: Who I Am	I need to be concerned with my growth as a person, not what jobs I do.
Depends on others' opinions		Not interested in popular opinion	I'll do what I know is right even if it's against popular opinion (Colossians 3:23).
Strives to earn and achieve		Realizes God gives character	I will build God's character in my life rather than strive to build my personal success.
Exclusive		Anyone	We all have the opportunity to be Christlike.
Quick to obtain		Slow process of growth	Important things will take a lot of time. I must learn patience.
Play the fool to maintain		Not dependent on success	I must be driven from the inside out, not the outside in.
Quick to lose		Strong in character	God wants to build things into my life that can't be taken away by anyone else.
God may take reputation away to build character		God will not take character away to build a reputation	God looks at the heart, not appearance!
Afraid of adversity		Survives adversity	I can see adversity as a way of life, a way for God to work and build character.

As we discussed these competing ethical systems, we became aware of some fairly serious implications for our respective ministries. We realized that if we genuinely desire to see the mighty hand of God on our ministry, we'd better make sure we don't program God out of our ministry or, worse, out of our personal lives. We need to eagerly anticipate the majesty and the mystery of God at work. For us it meant giving up some control to the Holy Spirit to make sure there was room for him to move. It meant scheduling our events a little looser; it meant being patient with gaps and allowing the element of surprise to be a welcome guest rather than a frightening intruder.

Effective youth workers know that sometimes the best youth ministry occurs when we're dependent on God. Maybe our preparation was interrupted so we really don't have the Bible study down, yet God moves in a miraculous way. Maybe a student comes with a huge burden and commands the attention you had planned to direct somewhere else. In both of these circumstances we're faced with abandoning or adjusting our plans to accommodate a situation we hadn't planned on. This often is God at work. He doesn't phone ahead to tell us what he's doing. He doesn't schedule an appointment: "I'll be at youth group Wednesday, and I'll move in a mighty way. Can you give me thirty minutes?"

I've noticed that God often works best when I'm experiencing what I call "divine irritation." I know it's supposed to be divine *intervention,* but it sometimes seems like more of an *irritation* to me because it affects my plans. I am the master of my youth group, the skipper of spirituality, the captain of the ship, and what I say goes; then God decides to cut in on my turf. That's when I get irritated. I actually have thought, "What is he doing here?! I didn't plan for this!"

It's at these times when I realize how insecure and weak I am. I'm using the youth group to fuel my personal needs because I've bought into the personality myth. My focus has shifted from "What does God want to do?" to "What will make me look good?" or "What do *I* want to do?" I could pity my weakness, but I realize that my weakness is an opportunity for God's strength. "In the same way, the Spirit helps us in our weakness. We do not know what we ought to pray for, but the Spirit himself intercedes for us with groans that words cannot express. And he who searches our hearts knows the mind of the Spirit, because the Spirit intercedes for the saints in accordance to God's will" (Romans 8:26-27).

Effective youth workers radiate the positive power of the Holy Spirit even when they're tired, weary, or feeling useless. They're able to do this because the energy doesn't come from them—it comes from the dynamics of the Holy Spirit within them. The Spirit is the energizer.

Late Night Cookies and Milk

We had been sleeping on the floor of a church classroom for five nights. Forty of us in one room—guys on one side, girls on the other. The snoring and other "night noises" were keeping me awake. As a veteran youth worker, I slept lightly so I could discern any late night activity, but my trained senses were working against me. I craved sleep; I was exhausted.

By day, we were youth on a mission—helping to establish a new church in a town a hundred miles from ours. It was hot, fatiguing work. I usually was the last to go to sleep and the first to wake up. Five hours of sleep per night wasn't enough to keep my flesh from kicking in and complaining. I was irritable, and I began questioning why I had come on this "stupid mission." I wondered why we couldn't go where they have beds.

I couldn't sleep, so I glanced around the room. I noticed that Kevin was awake and looking straight at me.

"Are you awake, Kevin?" I asked.

"Yeah, I can't sleep. You, too?" He seemed much more alert than I.

"Too much noise…do you want to go in the kitchen and get a snack?" I heard myself say. I couldn't believe my own words! Why was I all of a sudden gracious?

I thought, I want my rest. I deserve my rest. I can talk to Kevin tomorrow.

"Talk to him now," said a voice inside my head.

I don't feel up to it. I'm too tired and cranky, I told the voice.

"I will give you strength," said the voice.

I'll definitely need it, I thought in response. If you want me to talk with him, you'll have to give me strength and alertness, because I don't have it.

"In faith, act like you are energized by me," said the voice.

I stood and quietly stumbled into the kitchen. By the time I had poured a glass of milk and grabbed the cookies, I was totally awake.

Kevin began, "I really needed to talk. I just can't sleep. I need to talk with you about my Dad. I'm really worried about him, and I've never told anyone about this. Can we talk?"

I sensed God's presence in that room, and I realized God was the voice that had been speaking to me. As Kevin talked, I felt the positive power of God's Spirit begin to radiate within. I noticed I could listen and concentrate on what Kevin was saying. My body no longer felt tired, and I didn't need to sleep. Kevin opened up to me that night at a level which was very meaningful to both of us. It launched us into a close and significant relationship—one I would have missed if I had tried to relate to him in my strength. Because that night I didn't have strength; it all came from God. I was empty, and yet God used me. I learned that night that God uses our weakness to build bridges into the lives of other needy people. He uses our emptiness as opportunities to fill us with his grace. He uses our weariness as a backdrop for his mighty power, and he uses our dullness to awaken in us something much more conscious of the genuinely important. "'My grace is sufficient for you, for my power is made perfect in weakness.' Therefore, I will boast all the more gladly about my weaknesses, so that Christ's power may rest on me. That is why, for Christ's sake, I delight in weaknesses, in insults, in hardships, in persecutions, in difficulties. For when I am weak, then I am strong" (2 Corinthians 12:9-10).

Endnotes

1. John Ortberg, *The Life You've Always Wanted: Spiritual Disciplines for Ordinary People* (Grand Rapids, MI: Zondervan Publishing House, 1997), 75.

2. Stephen R. Covey, *The Seven Habits of Highly Effective People* (New York: Simon & Schuster, Inc., 1989), 19.

3. Oswald Chambers, *My Utmost For His Highest* (Grand Rapids, MI: Discovery House Publishers, 1992), August 4 Devotional. Emphasis added.

GROUP DISCUSSION QUESTIONS
Chapter 4: *Power Surge*
Nurture Your Soul by Radiating the
Positive Power of the Holy Spirit

1. Who stands out in your mind as being enthusiastic? What kind of impact has that person had on your life?

2. How do we, as youth workers, struggle with the personality myth? How does the motto "image is everything" affect us?

3. How do you feel about Oswald Chambers' words, "The most important aspect of Christianity is not the work we do, but the relationship we maintain"?

4. Discuss the contrasts between the Personality Ethic and the Character Ethic and the implications for ministry (p. 54).

5. Which of the issues you named in Question 4 do you struggle with? Explain.

6. Describe a time when God came through for you—when you experienced his strength in your weakness.

Developing Vision

*Nurture Your Soul by Believing
in Others and Their Growth*

Youth workers are people with vision. Who else would look at an obnoxious and disruptive twelve-year-old boy and believe someday God would really use him? This vision is faith in action; it's seeing what could be. It's not allowing our present parameters to determine our future horizons.

Rod was one of the most hyper junior high guys I had ever met. He talked constantly and always had some body part in motion. I dreaded having him in my cabin at camp because he never grew weary, in spite of that verse that says young men do grow weary.

I felt challenged to direct Rod's enormous amount of energy into something productive. I suggested long-distance running. He took it up, and, before I knew it, he was running five miles a day. In high school he went out for cross-country and became a star. He still was hyper at church, just a little more tired. I challenged Rod with being in student leadership, and he rose to the occasion and became an innovative, energetic leader in our youth group.

One of Rod's ideas was to play Ultimate Frisbee (Frisbee football) at ten thousand feet during our backpacking trip in California's High Sierras. It was a lot of fun playing on the tundra—someone would run for the Frisbee only to disappear in a hole of chilly water. Falling didn't hurt because of the mossy carpet. We were playing for the championships—my team against Rod's.

I had the Frisbee, and Rod was guarding me. The game was tied, one to one, and we had only a few more minutes to play.

I spied my teammate open in the end zone and forcefully snapped the Frisbee to him.

Rod was guarding me closely, and my hand caught him right in the nose and broke it. Rod bent over in pain, cradling his broken nose.

I felt terrible. I wanted to be able to stay ahead of this kid, not break his nose!

We grabbed some snow for his swollen face. I called the game, but Rod wanted to finish it. As we limped back to camp, he joked about how competitive I was that I would "break a kid's nose" to win. Then I realized why I believed in Rod. He was a lot like me. I saw in Rod the potential to be an effective leader. He had courage; he was persistent, self-disciplined, energetic, playful, and willful; and he'd make a perfect youth pastor! I believed in Rod and his growth. He wasn't perfect, but he was always in process. He seemed to have an accurate understanding of his strengths and weaknesses.

Like me, Rod often was criticized for being too rowdy and too radical. Today he's an effective youth pastor to a large youth group in Southern California. He's still rowdy, and he's a radical for God. I thank God for giving me the vision to see what could be in Rod.

Effective Youth Workers Are Visionaries

My working definition for *vision* is: an individual's specific mental image of what God wants to accomplish through him or her.

One of the key words in this definition is *specific*. Vision isn't some vague idea of a wish, it's a detailed picture of what God wants to accomplish. Another key word is mental. Vision requires imagination, concentration, and focus. And vision is an image—not a foggy, sketchy, impressionistic rendering, but a clear, definitive, objective portrait of what God seeks to do in the lives of people. This vision comes from God.

God's plans for this planet are too important to tolerate human-generated visions and schemes. God places his vision within the leaders he has chosen and gifted. Not every Christian has vision, but every effective Christian leader has vision.

Vision isn't simply "dreaming the impossible dream," to quote from the musical about Don Quixote; it's about dreaming the most *possible* dream. It is rooted in reality and then figures in the exponential factor of God-at-work, which leads to supernatural results.

An effective leader's vision has three essential aspects.

• It is specific.

• It is people-oriented.

• It positively embraces the future.

The Vision Is Specific

To lead people, a leader must have an idea of where he or she wants to go. A visionary youth worker has a specific mental image of a possible and desirable future for the youth ministry. This specific vision is essential because it defines both the future state and believable steps for how to get there. A specific vision motivates because it describes a condition that is better in some important ways than what now exists. A visionary youth worker provides the essential bridge from the present to a preferred future for the youth.

Roman Sanchez knows what he wants. As our middle school pastor, he has defined characteristics of a mature middle school student. These are the qualities he wants a student to have after spending three years in the MSM (middle school ministries). This desire becomes the vision of the entire middle school team. The team uses it to plan retreats, weekly programming, and individual discipleship. Not every student reflects these characteristics after being in the group, but many do. I have no doubt that many more students are developing these qualities than would if Roman hadn't shared his vision of a mature middle school student.

Specific vision motivates and guides. But a specific vision requires a clear picture of desired results and an action plan that details how to get there. God can work in dramatic ways, even within the brief three years of middle school.

The Vision Is People-Oriented

God's kingdom is built by people. He is a lover of people. His vision always involves his desire for people. God's vision for a youth worker will always involve using that youth worker to change the lives of people—the teenagers in the youth group. Changing lives is a priority—programs are important and buildings are helpful, but the vision involves life-change in people. If vision is people-oriented, then we must consider the needs felt by those we seek to serve and lead.

When the organization has a clear and common sense of purpose, direction, and desires for the future, individuals can find their own roles in the organization and in the larger society. This empowers individuals because they can see themselves as part of a worthwhile enterprise.[1]

When young people understand that they're a vital part of the vision, they gain a sense of importance. Effective youth workers help their teenagers—from the youngest middle school students to the most mature high school students—share the vision. The shared vision becomes the basis for a consensus about what's important in the youth ministry.

Great leaders inspire others to high levels of achievement by showing them how their work contributes to important causes. This is an emotional appeal to some of the most fundamental human needs—to be important, to make a difference, to feel useful, to be part of something important.[2]

Vision is important to people because it helps them meet some of their most basic needs of security, belonging, and significance, as well as challenging them to invest their lives in something of unparalleled importance—the kingdom of God.

Vision Positively Embraces the Future

An effective youth worker's vision always involves risk. Risk is an inherent part of vision because of the change required to reach the vision. Vision-led leaders refuse to be content with the status quo. They also refuse to be intimidated by an uncertain future. Instead of hiding from the future, a visionary will embrace it with confidence, knowing that the embrace will help shape it. Leaders are only as powerful as the ideas and vision they communicate. If they embrace the future with confidence and a passionate image of what can be, people will follow. To be effective youth workers, we need to be visionary leaders—out in front, thinking ahead of our youth, and helping them determine the future by building faith today.

"Leaders, in a special way, are liable for what happens in the future, rather than what happens day to day. This liability is difficult to measure, and thus the performance of leaders is difficult to measure. Though we do need to review past results and processes, the emphasis on the duties and performances of leaders has to be on the future. It is especially hard to remember that today's performance from a leader succeeds or fails only in the months or years to come. Much of a leader's performance cannot be reviewed until *after* the fact.

"Today's trust enables the future. We also enable the future by forgiving the mistakes we all make while growing up. We free each other to perform in the future through the medium of trust."[3]

The effective youth leader's vision is compassionate. It doesn't force people to stay stuck but allows them the freedom and the space to change. At the heart of this vision is the expectation that God will use us in the future in spite of our present weaknesses. Paul showed vision when he wrote about "Being confident of this, that He who began a good work in you will carry it to completion until the day of Christ Jesus" (Philippians 1:6).

Paul expected God to continue to work in spite of present circumstances. Paul was in prison when he wrote his letters to the Philippians, and he had every reason to be negative and pessimistic. Instead, he was hopeful and expectant. From his cell he could call to mind a specific image of what God wanted to accomplish through people to build God's kingdom. Paul provides us with an excellent example of vision as faith in action. His leadership challenged the inhibitors of God's vision. Vision builds on the past, but focuses on the future. It anticipates that God will be at work in ways we can imagine and in other ways we could never dream of. Vision empowers God's people emotionally and spiritually to move forward in faith.

Communicating Vision

Growth is more likely to occur in youth ministries that have developed a specific description of what they're trying to accomplish and have communicated that vision in such a way that everyone involved can share ownership of it. To the extent that a vision describes a desirable change in the future, it implies growth, which creates a feeling of expectancy—people expect that something is going to happen. This expectancy can be especially valuable in youth ministry because young people typically don't value routine and predictability. They prefer things to be dynamic and innovative.

When vision is understood and owned, it creates momentum and a feeling of accomplishment. Even before anything has actually happened, people feel a sense of accomplishment because they feel, "We're in this thing together, and we expect something to happen."

Teri was struggling with her youth group. She asked to talk with me after I spoke at a youth workers convention.

"I don't know what it is. I just feel bored with my youth group, and they act bored with me," she explained.

"What is it that you're trying to accomplish?" I asked.

"What do you mean?" she asked with a quizzical look.

"What are your goals? What would you like your youth group to look like after being with you for three years?"

"Well, I'm not sure. I guess I've just tried to entertain them and keep them out of trouble. I'm not sure they're ready for a challenge."

"Your lack of challenge is why you and they are bored. Coming to youth group could be so predictable that kids come expecting it to be dull. Growth is never boring. Describe in writing what you'd like God to do in the lives of your kids, share this with them, and ask for their help. I predict that you'll have an exciting group in one year if you do that."

A few years later I met Teri again, and she told me what had happened. "I left the convention determined to share my vision," she explained. "I realized I had been afraid of sharing my vision. I had it all along, but I thought the kids would alienate me if I shared it.

"Instead, they became motivated when I shared my dream for a loving, caring, active group which meets needs of people in and outside the group. We've taken trips to Mexico and to urban areas, and the group is even gearing up for the most frightening outreach—to the campus! It's really true that 'where there is no vision, the people perish.' Our youth group was dead; now it's alive!"

I smiled and asked, "Was there a cost to communicating the vision?"

"Sure, at first some of the kids didn't like the seriousness of our discussions, and they stopped coming. But most of them came back around when they saw that what we were doing was really significant and fun. All of a sudden it was cool to care; it used to be cool to be cold and rude."

"How did you communicate your vision?" I asked (always looking for ideas).

"We wrote a vision statement that captured in a sentence what we wanted to develop in our group. We wrote it on a large sign and hung it on the wall in our youth room. It was more than a slogan because the students helped write it. It took a long time and involved a lot of students, but now they own it. We studied several verses until we came up with a statement we all felt called to, felt challenged by, and could own. Our group has doubled in size in two years, and it's definitely not boring," beamed Teri.

Teri had learned the skill of communicating vision. She discovered that vision gives a youth ministry identity and shapes its culture. It sets the tone for how people work together and what they attempt to do. God supplies the vision. Teri had it all along, but she needed to let herself see it. Fear often keeps us from seeing the vision God has for us. Fear is the enemy of vision. God seeks to give us a Spirit that will fan the flame of our vision.

"For this reason I remind you to fan into flame the gift of God, which is in you through the laying on of my hands. For God did not give us a spirit of timidity but a spirit of power, of love and of self-discipline" (2 Timothy 1:6-7).

I see vision as a balance between power and love, with self-control providing support at the center.

The power side of the vision comes in response to the question, "What mighty work does God seek to do through me which is totally impossible unless he chooses to work?" And the weight of the power side prevents fear from eroding self-discipline and causing us to become defensive. Being afraid means that, instead of being self-disciplined, we're self-protective. Fear prevents us from understanding the vision God has for us.

On the other side of the balance is love vision. It is a response to the question, "Who needs to experience God's touch of love, healing, and grace?" God already has placed the gift within every believer, it's not our responsibility to fake the gift but to "fan into flame the gift" God has placed in us.

Don't fake it—fan it!

Focus Shift

Insecurity can cause us to concentrate on the wrong things, and this focus can be intimidating. If what we're looking at scares us into inactivity and timidity, we need to shift our focus from
- program to people,
- production to principles,
- past to future,
- obstacles to opportunities, and
- fear of criticism to cultural relevance.

If we're going to challenge youth with a vision of significance and community, we'll need to look past our **program** into the eyes of the **people** we work with. We'll need to focus more on **principles** and less on **production**—what we're doing and creating. We might need to take some time-out to think and reflect and actually not *do* something.

In a principled paradigm, behavior and potential can be seen as two different things. As a result, the principled youth worker refuses to judge, label, categorize, or stereotype people. He or she sees within each individual the limitless capacity of God's grace. A principled youth worker doesn't have to overreact to negative behaviors, criticism, or human weakness. Understanding that potential is a process, not a point, is a liberating perspective that allows the youth worker to visualize growth and potential in others. It also points a search for significance into the **future** rather than the **past**.

Pity the youth worker who judges his or her worth on the last big success.

Opportunities—some call them **obstacles**—surround the visionary youth worker. Being an opportunist, the visionary youth worker can see these "obstacles" as stones that will become steppingstones and, later, milestones.

Many youth workers get stuck in the **fear of criticism**—both real and imagined. It takes courage to be **relevant to a changing culture**. It's safe to maintain a "sanctification mind-set" which says, "Let's not be too relevant or else we'll be too worldly and become tainted." There's risk in reaching people with needs, but, if they didn't have real needs, why would they need a Savior?

It was in the early days of punk. I was a youth pastor at the Evangelical Free Church in Fresno, California. It was a conservative church in a conservative town, and there was a conservative church board to keep an eye on things. I liked the refreshing honesty and angst I found in punk, so I invited a new, cutting-edge Christian band to do a Wednesday night concert.

OK, so Wednesday was a bad night to choose; it was family night. We had choir, Awana Club for kids, a variety of classes for adults, our youth programs, and, of course, the church board meeting.

I made some flyers and spread them around town. We were expecting two hundred students, but more than eight hundred showed up! I guess this neophyte band, Undercover, was a draw! You should have seen the Awana kids' eyes when the parking lot turned into Purple Mohawks on Parade!

The church board members were not amused when they heard Undercover's intensity and volume. They were four buildings and 150 yards away, but they heard the concert. Parents thought the youth group had gone to hell on a skateboard when they dropped their kids off. I never knew we had that many punks in Fresno. We had a few in the youth group, but who would have guessed there were hundreds?

That night, more than one hundred kids responded to Joey Taylor's invitation to become Christians—most of them kids we'd never have reached with our preppie program. I received enough complaints to wallpaper my office with phone messages and letters. But I learned a lesson that made it worth it all—being culturally relevant requires the courage to take criticism. That was the beginning of a long string of concerts.

Focusing In

It's impossible to meet all the needs of youth in your community. You need to decide *which* needs you'll meet. Ask yourself, "What needs am I burdened with? Which are we uniquely qualified to meet? What might our niche be? Which of these needs makes me pound the table with passion?" Then ask yourself, "Why do we exist? What is our mission statement?" To help you in this process, look at the diagram on page 69.

The Calvary Rocket is a planning tool I use to communicate vision and develop goals. I start from the top and work down. After we've determined our *purpose,* we need to ask ourselves how we're different from other youth ministries in town. We've determined we're "Christ-centered, biblically based, culturally relevant, and outreach-oriented." This makes us quite different from other significant ministries in our area, but it's us. It makes us distinctive.

Under *objectives,* we're looking for broad categories of ministries we know we'll always do, such as Bible study, evangelism, caring, and discipleship. We then seek to define our vision and describe it in writing as our *dreams.* Finally, we record our steps toward the dreams as our *goals.*

Vision needs to be specific. If we don't have a clearly defined vision, we'll try to meet all the needs of all the youth in our community. Vision limits by being specific, but it also liberates. We don't have to do everything.

Could it be that God might use another youth ministry in the community to build his kingdom? Vision is a specific picture of what God wants to do.

Because vision is specific, it's also personal. A well-written vision statement includes actual people. Notice the contrast between these two vision statements:

A. My vision is to live for Jesus.

B. My vision is to prepare as many people as possible for Christ's return.

Our church vision is B. Once we defined our vision, we wanted to make it personal, practical, and memorable, but we weren't sure how. Since we live near Los Angeles, we often see graffiti sprayed on the walls of buildings and freeways. I guess you could say that "tagging" is part of our culture. Someone suggested that we make our vision intensely personal.

"Why don't we make a giant banner with our vision on it and hang it on the wall? Then we can write on the wall all the names of friends and family we're trying to reach, the ones we want to see become Christians and prepare for his return."

THE CALVARY ROCKET

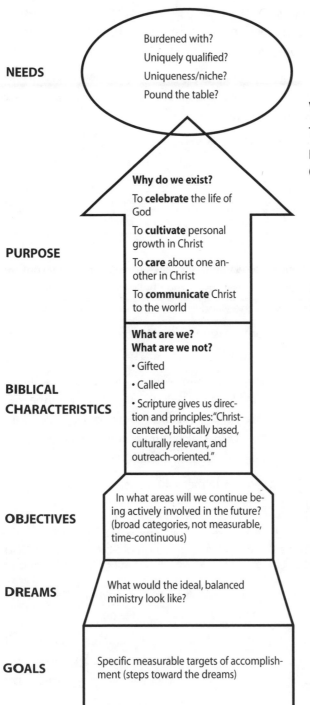

NEEDS

Burdened with?
Uniquely qualified?
Uniqueness/niche?
Pound the table?

VISION:

To prepare as many people as possible for Christ's return.

PURPOSE

Why do we exist?
To **celebrate** the life of God

To **cultivate** personal growth in Christ

To **care** about one another in Christ

To **communicate** Christ to the world

BIBLICAL CHARACTERISTICS

What are we?
What are we not?

• Gifted

• Called

• Scripture gives us direction and principles: "Christ-centered, biblically based, culturally relevant, and outreach-oriented."

OBJECTIVES

In what areas will we continue being actively involved in the future? (broad categories, not measurable, time-continuous)

DREAMS

What would the ideal, balanced ministry look like?

GOALS

Specific measurable targets of accomplishment (steps toward the dreams)

At this time we were beginning a campaign to purchase new property. The theme of the campaign became "The Wall." We began listing names of people we wanted to see in a relationship with Christ. We listed only their first names: James, Susan, Harvey, Claude, Jennifer…

We asked people to record these names on their Bible bookmarks and pray for them also. After a few weeks, thousands of names were listed on the wall. We were amazed with the response.

The plan was visionary.

It was personal.

It was practical.

It was powerful.

It worked!

The scope of our church's vision is to reach ten percent of our community for Christ. About two hundred thousand people live in the area. Our vision challenges us to reach twenty thousand people!

Some people thought the vision was far-fetched.

The wall wound up with about twenty-five thousand names listed from the floor to the ceiling. We have a team that actually counts and prays for each one. When a person whose name is on the wall becomes a Christian, the friend who wrote the name places a red apple sticker next to the name. For us an apple represents new life. It looks like we're making strides toward reaching this huge vision. Hundreds of apples now dot the wall!

We've discovered a literal truth that "where there is no vision, the people perish" (Proverbs 29:18, KJV).

Our vision—to have an impact on our community for Christ—is beyond our power. It's impossible without the mighty power of God. Believing in God-size visions demands dependence on God.

The best vision statement doesn't guarantee anything. We must be intentional about using our statement to evaluate all we do.

Consider the words of best-selling business authors, James C. Collins and Jerry I. Porras, in their book, *Built To Last: Successful Habits of Visionary Companies:* "Yes, it's very important to stop and think about vision. But even more important, you have to align the organization to preserve the core ideology and stimulate progress toward the envisioned future, not merely write a statement. Keep in mind that there is a big difference between being an organization with a vision statement and becoming a truly visionary organization. When you have superb alignment, a visitor could drop into your organization from another planet and infer the vision without having to read it on paper."[4]

The Calvary Rocket planner is only one way of describing the vision and the steps required to implement it. Vision is a specific mental image of what God wants to accomplish through you to build his kingdom. We need tools like this to build. We also need a team of builders.

The "Empower" Team

Vision is crucial if you're going to be effective in youth ministry. But you can't do it alone; you'll need a team of people who share the vision. Following are ten tips for empowering your team with vision:

1. Develop a vision statement that captures your vision.
2. Regularly communicate your vision statement to your team.
3. Expect the best from your team members.
4. Know the needs of your students and team members.
5. Establish high standards of excellence.
6. Learn from failure.
7. Promote team spirit (minimize competition).
8. Encourage and model personal renewal.
9. Celebrate achievement and growth.
10. Balance ministry with the rest of your life (be able to say no).

"So from now on we regard no one from a worldly point of view. Though we once regarded Christ in this way, we do so no longer. Therefore, if anyone is in Christ, he is a new creation; the old is gone, the new has come!" (2 Corinthians 5:16,17).

Endnotes

1. Warren Bennis and Burt Nanus, *Leaders* (New York: Harper and Row Publishers, Inc., 1985), 91.

2. Bennis and Nanus, *Leaders,* 93.

3. Max DePree, *Leadership Is an Art* (New York: Dell Publishing, Inc., 1989), 114-115.

4. James C. Collins and Jerry I. Porras, *Built to Last: Successful Habits of Visionary Companies* (New York: HarperBusiness, 1994), 239.

GROUP DISCUSSION QUESTIONS
Chapter 5: *Developing Vision*
Nurture Your Soul by Believing in Others and Their Growth

1. How have you seen potential in a student before that person discovered it?

2. Early in this chapter, the author said, "Vision is faith in action; it's seeing what could be. It's not allowing our present parameters to determine our future horizons." Why is vision essential for effective youth work?

3. Discuss why vision has to
   be specific
   be people-oriented
   positively embrace the future.

4. Why are leaders liable for what happens in the future?

5. Why is vision necessary for nurturing your soul?

6. Discuss the Calvary Rocket planner (p. 69). How could you utilize this planning tool for your youth ministry?

7. Develop some practical steps for applying the ten tips for empowering your team with vision (p. 71).

The Balancing Act

Nurture Your Soul With Balance

"What kinda pop, mon?" asked the Caribbean storekeeper.

"What kind is there?" I replied, hoping for something new.

"Pepsi, Marinda…Pepsi," he said as his chilled hand fished in the cooler's melting ice water.

Two choices—Marinda, which is an orange-flavored soda, and the old standby, Pepsi. I was thirsty for a Mountain Dew, but on Roatan Island, thirty miles north of mainland Honduras, we were lucky to have chilled Pepsi. Every afternoon, after I had taught school, taken my siesta, and coached soccer, I made my pilgrimage to the store. I was disappointed in the lack of variety, but there was something comforting about the ritual. I would ask for something, the store-keeper would say he didn't have it, I'd buy something else, and I'd leave content. The people of Roatan didn't have much, but they were content.

Then, after 365 such episodes, it was time to return to California.

For me, the culture shock was worse when I came home than when I went overseas. My first trip to the supermarket threw me into a panic: Pepsi, Coke, Dr Pepper, root beer, 7Up, orange soda, *and* Mountain Dew! Too many choices! I was overwhelmed by the toilet paper aisle—mountains of toilet paper in a mind-boggling assortment of colors, sheets, plies, and textures. On Roatan we were happy to have the rough tan stuff that resembled plywood. I was stressed by the choices. I was psychologically fatigued by the options presented to me. I was on "overload"—and I was only shopping.

As we sprint into the new millennium, most of us live in a constant state of choosing. Life is a multiple-choice test. Even television was simpler when all we had to watch were the three networks. Now, with cable and satellite, we have hundreds of choices. It takes so much time, energy, and focus just to make it through the rudimentary choices of the day.

Upon returning to California, I felt concerned about the waste going into trivial decisions. It seemed to me people were stressed by the pace of life and were on "decision overload." I longed for the simple days on the island where the pace of life allowed time to chat with the folks and sip a Pepsi.

Pace and product are the beat of the day. Our culture attaches value to a busy person—we assume that person must be important. Achievement is another source of affirmation in our culture. "Just Do It" is more than a slogan for shoes; it's a national creed.

Pressure comes from a society that *values being hurried.* We have grown accustomed to having everything *now.* We tell a sign behind a restaurant what we want for dinner, then we expect it to be prepared by the time we pull our car around to the window. Automatic teller machines give us instant cash. Microwaves give us quick meals. Modern malls give us instant debt. We're in a love affair with haste. [1]

Being a youth worker in the age of haste is challenging and reactions to this challenge can vary between two extremes. On one hand we have "911 Nancy" who responds at all hours to all calls for help. She is a seven-day-a-week youth worker. Her husband and children just have to understand she is "doing God's work…they can wait."

At the other extreme is "Phil Family Man." He announced to his church, "I can only be out two nights a week. My first priority is my family." Phil had heard this idea at a conference and decided to try it out. It did give him more time with his wife and infant son, but the youth group suffered because of his lack of availability.

Nancy and Phil illustrate the pull toward polar extremes when we lose the balance in our lives.

Paul Borthwick offers three balancing acts we need to achieve if we're to be effective:[2]

- personal time versus ministry time,
- thought time versus activity time,
- time with adults versus time with students.

I'd like to add a fourth:

- time with parents versus time with youth.

Personal Time Pressures

I never used to struggle with the tension of personal time versus ministry time, and that was a problem. If something needed to get done, I'd carve out time to do it. That time came out of my personal time. At one point I was working seventy hours a week: teaching junior high, high school, and college each twice a week; attending games on Fridays; hosting youth events on Saturdays; attending numerous meetings all week. And I was feeling pretty positive about myself. I was important because I was busy. I was valuable because I produced. "Who else could teach three different lessons to three different age groups in three consecutive hours every Sunday? I am capable and worthwhile," I told myself. I missed countless quiet evenings with my wife.

"There's the lock-in," I protested.

My daughter's first words were uttered while I was gone. "We always go to Mexico for a week. It's crucial; it's a mission," I rationalized.

My wife and I had issues to face and conversations that needed to take place, but I didn't have the time for them. I was too busy. I used to think I was running *to* something, but I was running *from* something. I stayed so busy because I thought I needed to succeed—I was running from failure.

In high school and college, I was a runner. Competition meant running harder and longer. I learned that to win you need to work harder and faster. When I applied this philosophy to youth ministry, I got results.

My youth group grew to hundreds. People affirmed me for the results. The youth group gained a very favorable reputation in the city. People offered to be on staff—I had a waiting list. Church members offered us their cabins, boats, recreation vehicles, and Palm Springs condos. Many regularly donated money for our scholarship fund. The church leaders gave me a promotion, a larger office, and a raise. I was asked to write articles and speak on "The Elements of Success-ful Youth Ministry." Results—there you have it: I was a success.

Or was I?

Nobody, I mean *nobody,* ever asked me, "Tim, do you think you're working too much?" or "How are things at home? Are you balancing your time with your family?"

Looking back, it makes me fearful to see how unbalanced I was. It also makes me angry—why didn't anyone say anything? Couldn't they see that my life was out of balance? I kept running harder and faster. I was still competing. Instead of braking my frenzied pace, the church affirmed it. I needed a church leader to question me about my family life; instead, each one applauded my productivity.

I've observed that churches sometimes do more to fuel compulsive behav-ior than to heal it. It's a blurry line between biblical servant and co-dependent en-abler. But that's nothing new. Since the exit from Eden, sin has refused to let us rest. Our frantic pace is a result of taking shortcuts in life. Sin wears many dis-guises, but in the nude it's the passion to have it all now. Our natural drives lead us to an overloaded life.

We believe such lies as "bigger is better," "worth equals net worth" and "busy-ness is next to Godliness." In order to feel better about ourselves, we spend more effort on our ministry. Meanwhile, our primary relationships at home suffer be-cause of neglect. Hurry becomes our master.

John Ortberg offers a warning in *The Life You've Always Wanted.* He writes, "It is because it kills love that hurry is the great enemy of spiritual life. Hurry lies be-hind much of the anger and frustration of modern life. Hurry prevents us from receiving love from the Father or giving it to His children. That's why Jesus never hurried. If we are to follow Jesus, we must ruthlessly eliminate hurry from our lives—because, by definition, we can't move faster than the one we are following.

"We can do this: We can become unhurried people. We can become patient people."[3]

I like the idea of not moving faster than the one we're following. Hurrying can become a form of idolatry. We place our schedule, our activities, and our work ahead of our Lord. We shouldn't move faster than the one we're following.

Thought time versus activity time

Youth work creates a tension between being with students and being alone so you have something to offer when you're with them. We tend to favor one over the other: study time or student time.

Dave is a highly relational youth worker. He's got the trendy haircut and the stylish sports car, and he dresses in vogue. In a word, Dave is "cool." Most of his time is spent eating with kids, listening to CD's, going to concerts, or just hangin' with them.

Dave has a difficult time studying for the Bible study. He'd rather be relational than academic. Balance for Dave means reading a Christian book for an hour every week, spending an hour studying the Bible, and spending an hour preparing the lesson. These three hours are difficult for Dave, but this is the balance he needs. He asked his boss to hold him accountable for these three hours.

Julie is an analytical youth worker. She likes to study trends among adolescents and think about her particular students. She is most content in her office, reading a journal on adolescent behavior. She likes to study, plan, dream, and think. She's an expert on the computer and uses desktop publishing to create some high-quality graphics. She maintains nine-to-five office hours and is there most of the time. If students want to see her, they can call and make an appointment. Julie needs to balance her thought time with some activity. She has decided to spend three afternoons out of the office and go where her students are—games, the mall, rehearsals, and workouts—where they work and where they relax.

Time with adults versus time with students

Spending all our time with students makes for tired and immature youth workers. We need to be around other adults who will challenge us to grow and, in some cases, serve us. Youth workers who spend all their time with students expose themselves to the risk of losing their balance and perspective.

Tom loved to spend time with guys in his small group. Since he was single, he spent every weekend with them. After a while, I noticed Tom was beginning to act like a teenager. He was having difficulty relating to his peers on the youth team, and he began to lose his objective perspective on the kids.

One of the guys in his small group was developing a serious drinking problem, but Tom was defensive and made excuses for this teenager. As a result of this imbalance, Tom began to lose credibility with the other adult volunteers and be the subject of serious questions from parents of the guys in his small group.

One parent pointed out, "It seems like Tom needs the students more than they need him." This sent up the flares for me. I got together with Tom and told him about the parent's comment. Then we developed a plan to balance his life. I asked him to spend two weekends a month and two nights a week with friends in the twenty-something singles group.

Tom's friends were glad to see him back, and Tom discovered a sense of balance, perspective, and freedom he had lost.

I asked some of the high school guys in his group what they thought about the "new Tom," and one of them said, "It's better now that Tom has a life!"

Of course, the other extreme is to be like Julie by barricading yourself in your office or home and not spending time with students. When Julie forced herself to hang out with kids, she discovered a renewed understanding of kids that you can't get from a journal. After her youth group members introduced her to their friends and parents, she was able to teach more effectively because she could picture their world with much more detail and understanding. Her credibility skyrocketed with the students because they sensed she cared.

Time with parents versus time with students

This never used to be a tension for youth workers—it was a given, spend the time with the kids. But now things are different. It used to be that we would see kids come to youth events three times a week and on weekends. Those days are gone. Our time with teenagers is minimized. Many young people are too busy to come to a youth event more than once a week.

How can we have an impact on a generation of busy teens? We can touch their lives through their parents. If we minister to the parents, we'll increase the impact we have on the home. When we acknowledge that our kids come from family systems, we will seek to support and influence those systems, rather than focus simply on individuals in the systems.

Most youth workers are afraid of parents. They see parents as problems, not people. They're afraid that, if they get involved with parents, they'll lose control of the youth ministry or the youth will feel betrayed.

Steve was a popular youth worker who had been at his church for five years. Some of the graduates had come back to help in the youth ministry. They liked Steve and were glad to be back in the youth group—but this time they were staff.

Steve's ministry to parents consisted of an annual parents meeting, at which he handed out calendars and coffee and discussed the year's schedule. He was afraid more interaction with parents would give them more opportunity to complain or criticize. He wanted to play it safe; he wanted to keep control. He wanted to keep his distance from parents.

Steve enjoyed working with his staff; he was older than them by only a few years. They liked the same TV programs and tended to have the same style of humor—*Saturday Night Live* meets David Letterman. Working with this gang made youth ministry fun. After a while, parents began to question the "depth of his teaching" and the "lack of emphasis on discipleship."

Mr. Major, a leader in the church and an adult Sunday school teacher, was concerned that his daughter, Melody, wasn't involved with the youth group. He made her go when she was in junior high, but he felt she should have the choice when she got to high school. She chose not to go. When encouraged to attend, she would respond, "The youth group is cliquish, and Steve is boring." Mr. Major shared his concern with some other parents over coffee before Sunday school. Some of them had teenagers who didn't like going to youth group. The more they talked, the more critical and negative they became. Before they had finished their second cup of coffee, some of the parents were thinking about replacing Steve as youth pastor.

Mr. Major scheduled an appointment with the senior pastor and shared his concerns regarding the "lack of maturity, depth, and breadth" of Steve's ministry. He told the pastor, "Several of us church members and leaders are considering leaving the church to find a ministry that meets the needs of our teenagers."

Pastor Warner had seen this type of spiritualized manipulation before and didn't fall into Mr. Major's trap. "Have you talked to Steve about this?" he asked. "I'm sure he'd benefit from being aware of your concerns."

"No, we haven't," explained Mr. Major. "Isn't that your job?"

"The Bible says if you have a concern with your brother you need to go directly to him. I think you need to go directly to Steve. To avoid him is to promote discord which hurts the unity of the body," admonished the wise pastor.

Mr. Major sheepishly agreed to talk to Steve.

Steve listened to Mr. Major's complaints and asked, "Are you concerned with the spiritual maturity of the youth group?"

"Why yes," replied Mr. Major, "That's why I'm here."

"Then you would say we need to pray for these kids?" asked Steve.

"Of course, they need our support," agreed Mr. Major.

"Then would you be willing to help organize a parents' prayer support team for our youth ministry?"

"Yeah, sure. What would it require?"

"I'll prepare a monthly newsletter to inform your team of prayer requests and praises for answered prayer. You get together with parents to pray for our youth group, the staff, and me."

Six months later, Steve still had his job. He also had a team of fourteen parents committed to pray for him, his staff, and the youth. Steve discovered a principle for effective youth ministry: Involve the parents in what you're doing. Not only did Steve have a parents' support team (PST), but he also began to include parents in events, errands, and camps. They provided much of the labor-intensive work and freed up the staff to be relational with the students. As parents barbecued hot dogs, they could observe their teenagers developing relationships with the youth staff. When the parents met together and prayed, they began to compare notes about their kids. Some of the kids had legitimate concerns about the youth group, but many of them were using the complaints to "get back at" their parents. They knew they could get a reaction from their parents.

Mr. Major and other parents told their kids, "The youth group isn't perfect, but it's our youth group, and we need to support it. You need to go and give it another chance. Let Steve know what you think we can do to improve it, and give him the opportunity to address your concerns."

Parents and youth workers can work together. I'm realizing that a ministry to and with parents is essential. If we include parents, they tend to work with us; when we don't, they tend to work against us. Jesus said something about that: "He who is not with me is against me."

Myths That Lead to Imbalance

I was presenting a seminar for parents in North Carolina. I noticed that some of the parents were beginning to fade and think about lunch. I decided to re-capture their attention.

"We're going to break for lunch in a few minutes, but I want to warn you about the iced tea. During the break, I sneaked over to the kitchen and poured eight ounces of poison into the five-gallon container of iced tea. OK, now back to parenting. A myth is something that seems true but is tainted by a little falseness. It's mostly true and feels comfortable and familiar, but it has just enough false in it to taint the whole batch. A myth is like the iced tea—it looks good and tastes good, but, if we ingest it, it will bring us trouble. Let's break for lunch. After we eat, we will talk about myths."

At lunch, a funny thing happened. The coordinator of the citywide seminar was sitting at my table. As he reached for some potato chips, he knocked over his iced tea—all twenty ounces of it. People teased him about drinking the "poisoned cup." He claimed my story made him nervous, but he cleaned everything up, got another plate of food, and sat down to eat. Then he noticed the center-piece was out of place. As he moved it to the center of the table, he knocked over a tumbler full of tea, and it splattered all over me. Parents were rolling with laughter. The jokes and the teasing made it a very enjoyable lunch. I'm not sure those parents will remember the six-hour seminar on parenting, but they will remember the story of the poisoned iced tea!

The dangerous myths are the ones that are only partially false. Placing confidence in a belief that is somewhat less than true gives us a shaky foundation for our assumptions. Let's take a look at some myths in youth work that lead to imbalance.

Myth 1: Youth workers don't work with parents.

As was discussed earlier, being effective with teenagers requires relating to the family systems they come from.

Myth 2: You have to earn the right to be heard.

I know this is a popular slogan for youth ministry, but it can be taken to an extreme. I know because I spent two years trying to be cool and build friendships before I ever mentioned God, let alone sin or other serious topics. Teenagers want us to be relational, but they *need* us to be intentional.

Myth 3: Teenagers want fun, not substance.

This is mostly true—no teenagers want boredom. But most want significance. They're looking for credible responses to the question, "So what?" It's a lot easier to begin with something that is inherently significant and add fun than to start with something fun and seek to add significance.

Dewey Bertolini encourages youth workers to choose activities based on your purpose. The purpose needs to be clear in all we do in youth work.

"If you establish the purposes first and choose activities based on the purposes, you'll see the following results: you and the entire staff will feel a sense of achievement as you meet the clearly defined goals, you'll experience the thrill of meeting specific needs in the lives of the young people, the young people will learn to discern and model our achievement orientation as they see a goal accomplished, the activity calendar will have a sense of balance since every event centers on a comprehensive list of purposes, you'll have avoided the leading cause of youth ministry burnout—the expenditure of time and energy with nothing lasting to show for it, and you'll be following the most important programming priority: *Do nothing without meaning!*" [4]

Myth 4: You have to act like one of them.

Teenagers are looking for someone who understands them, not someone who acts like them. They want someone they can look up to, not across to. Many youth workers have mistaken being relational with being immature. They have believed the myth that says, "To relate to teenagers you must demonstrate teenager-like behavior." Some teenagers have told me these are the youth workers they despise. Teenagers need models who walk ahead of them, who guide them. Guides who get too far ahead are difficult to relate to and keep up with, but those who play around and get lost on the journey won't inspire much confidence in their followers. Teenagers choose not to follow adults who act like adolescents.

Myth 5: You must relate and teach from your strength.

A common maxim in ministry has been that you should utilize your strengths and staff to your weakness. In other words, do what you're best at and look for others to complement your weaknesses. This maxim may be true in staffing, but it doesn't work as well for spiritual growth.

I used to think my youth group needed to see me as a spiritual knight, ready and able to take on the dragons of this world. I wanted to present to the teenagers a capable, successful strongman. But taking a deeper look at myself showed me that this image wasn't very authentic. I struggle with insecurity, fear of rejection, and fear of failure. I realized I needed to share some of my weakness if I was to be genuine and authentic. Early experiments with relating from a point of weakness opened the hearts of many in the group. I'm learning that relating from a position of strength can build barriers while relating from a position of weakness often builds bridges into the lives and hearts of our youth.

Myth 6: Don't show emotion.

This myth is similar to the previous one in that it promotes being less than we really are. Somehow we have bought into the notion that the more mature we are the less emotion we show. We have wrongly equated demonstration of emotion with immature behavior. Teenagers are emotional, and they're looking for adults who can show them how to deal with their emotions. Denying we have emotions, such as fear, doubt, anger, and sadness, robs us of the opportunity to build bridges into the hearts of the teenagers in our group.

I used to believe in the "don't show emotion" myth. I thought my youth group would feel I was "too weak" or "not a man" if I shared my emotions. Anger was the only emotion I felt like displaying. It's OK for a man to be angry, but admitting I was lonely or sad would make me too vulnerable.

I taught many fine lessons from the Bible, but I don't think they had much of an impact on the youth. The lessons were food for thought. My goal was to teach content, to help youth comprehend the truth of God's word. I prided myself on how we had progressed through the Old and New Testaments and how the students had learned how to study the Bible on their own. But something was missing—the passion and the excitement were fading.

Then I heard someone say, "A lesson prepared in the head reaches heads. A lesson prepared in the heart reaches hearts. A lesson prepared in a life reaches lives." I realized I had been preparing only in my head. I wasn't sure how to prepare my life to reach lives, but I decided to share my life—my struggles, my joys, my confusion, and my ambivalence—as a part of my teaching. As I became more authentic about my emotions, my lessons became more colorful. The hues and tints of real life began to show. I had been teaching in black and white; adding emotion allowed me to teach in color. I discovered that teaching to the heart as well as the head allowed me to reach people at a much deeper level.

Myth 7: Don't delegate—they'll blow it.

This myth is easy to believe because so much evidence and experience supports its truth. But this myth will bring death to effective youth work. If youth workers wrongly assume that they must do it if they want it done right, they'll become very controlling and tired people.

After all, ministry is about serving others, and people grow best when they're serving. We need to share the serving so others can grow. Sure, they may not do the job as well as we could—but the point is progress, not perfection. The wise youth worker knows what he or she can delegate and does so. He or she also works with a net. Just as a tightrope walker has a net underneath, so does an effective youth worker. We create a safety net to catch people when they fall. People will fail and will fall, but they won't be destroyed. People learn much from failing, and they shouldn't be robbed of the lessons that can be learned only from failure. At the same time, an effective leader won't let followers feel like failures.

I have observed that students and staff are very teachable after they fail with an assignment. We don't need to fix blame, but we do need to learn from the failure. I tell my student leaders and staff, "If we can learn from it, it's not a failure unless we try to blame someone." Taking a critical look at something and fine-tuning it helps us pursue excellence. But it takes failure to fully develop excellence. Mediocrity can happen without failure, but achieving excellence requires learning the lessons that come from making mistakes. We empower people to serve when we trust them with the ministry. I like to challenge my team to entrust the ministry to student leaders. I tell them, "The same Holy Spirit that is in you is in them!"

The Rhythm Method of Youth Work

No, I'm not advocating a birth control schedule! I'm talking about the natural rhythms that occur in every youth group. The effective youth worker senses the rhythm of the group because he or she notices certain patterns. Nature provides us with many examples. Picture the tides coming in and going out each day. A high tide is good for launching a boat; a low tide is good for skimboarding. Seasoned youth workers notice similar "tidal" changes in their youth groups. There will be times of high-tide excitement followed by low-tide blues. The right time to launch a ministry could depend on the "tide" of your group.

Groups also have seasons. You may be experiencing winter with a frigid, unresponsive group that keeps to itself and doesn't venture out. Following your Easter outreach trip, you may experience a spring thaw and rebirth as students become excited about reaching out. In the summer of your group, you may notice a desire for resting and building relationships. The autumn of your group may involve some changes. Just as leaves turn colors and drop, some of your "leaves" may change. Of course, the seasons of a youth ministry aren't necessarily connected to the four seasons, but in some cases they are. Study your group and look for its natural rhythms. This understanding will help you balance your ministry because you will discover "there is a time and a season for everything under the sun." Knowing what season it is will bring balance to youth work.

A balanced youth worker has developed a sense of equilibrium regarding time. The youth worker has been able to reconcile the four major competitive time demands:

• Personal time versus ministry time
• Thought time versus activity time
• Time with adults versus time with students
• Time with parents versus time with students

Study the diagram, "Balanced Time = Effectiveness," on the next page. Picture the center of the circle being horizontal and balanced on a pin, like a plate spinning on a stick. Balance in youth ministry can be that tricky.

Evaluate your personal ministry balance by shading in each pie slice to the degree you spend time there. For instance, if you spend a lot of time with students, shade one of the pieces labeled "students." Notice the corresponding slice, which could be time with parents or time with adults. If you spend time with your adult friends, shade the "adult" piece according to your estimation of how much time you spend with your friends. If you never spend time with the parents of students, leave that piece unshaded.

After you shade the pieces, you'll have a graphic representation of how you

Balanced Time=Effectiveness

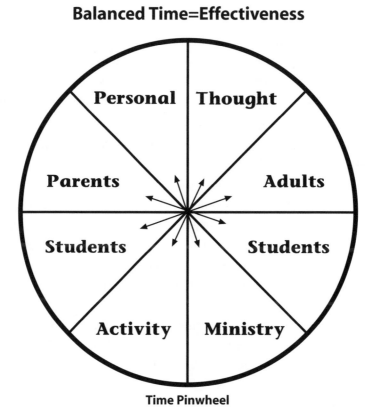

Time Pinwheel

spend your time. Evaluate whether this time balance reflects your priorities. If it does, you have a pinwheel that will affirm you. Each youth worker will have different priorities for time. There is no "right answer" for all youth workers. The point of the Time Pinwheel is to make us aware of the competing time demands that exist in youth work and to see if we're balanced in handling them.

When you go for a medical checkup, the doctor does a variety of diagnostic tests to see if you're healthy. People vary in their responses to the individual tests. Your resting pulse might be sixty-four beats per minute while another person's might be eighty. To determine whether a person is in good health, a doctor considers many variables. A healthy body is balanced. And a healthy youth worker seeks to maintain balance by holding himself and herself accountable to a sensible pace and schedule.

The Personal Pathology of the Youth Worker

A sense of pace, balance, and accountability will help a youth worker stay healthy and effective. But what is it that causes many of us to "crash and burn"? I'd like to suggest six common vices of youth workers, which I call the "Six L's Down."

1. Lack of accountability

I used to meet with Lee (not his real name) for lunch. We'd trade ideas, share resources, and encourage each other in youth ministry. Occasionally we'd plan events together. Lee was an articulate, passionate, and dynamic youth pastor. He never told me he and his wife, Cherie, were having problems. I thought they had it all together—large church, new house, new car, healthy children, and an ample salary. People in his church were pleased with his effective ministry and were settling into the idea of Lee and Cherie being at First Church for a long time. But midway into his third year, Lee was fired for having an affair with a woman in the church. The youth group was devastated. The church was shocked. Cherie was crushed beyond recovery, and she left Lee.

I was stunned by the exposé. I'd had no inkling of Lee's adulterous behavior. I felt betrayed and angry. "How could he do this to everyone?" I wanted to know. Lee and I had spent dozens of hours together—but not once had we asked each other any of the *hard* questions, such as,

Are you still in the Word?

Do you have a heart for Jesus?

How are you feeling about God?

How are things with your wife?

Do you find yourself looking outside your marriage for satisfaction?

When was the last time you and your wife got away for a romantic weekend?

How can I pray for you, confidentially, about your marriage?

Have you benefited from marriage counseling?

I didn't ask the hard questions. I didn't think about it then; now I do. I don't think any of us can afford not to. The problem is we're *more comfortable being peace keepers than truth tellers.* We'd rather convince ourselves we're "keeping the peace" by being superficial, protective, and avoiding accountability.

No one grows best without truth. No one is pushed to be the best. And from a Christian perspective, men and women never will be all that God wants them to be unless they're faced with the truth. [5]

To become all God has intended us to be we need to be accountable for our balance of time and our personal purity and holiness. I've chosen to meet weekly with two mature Christian men who hold me accountable by asking me the hard questions. I think they've helped me in a way I wished I had helped Lee.

Paul Borthwick wrote that, after seeing the fall of two spiritual mentors, he decided that he "needed an accountability partner. Someone who would ask me hard questions, keep me from bluffing, and hold my feet to the fire concerning my spiritual growth. Axiom: Spiritual health demands a friend who will walk alongside us, speak truth to us (even when it hurts), and keep us honest in our relationships with God and with other people."[6]

2. Loneliness

Rick is one of the guys in my support group. He was relatively new to our church when he walked up to me one Sunday morning and asked, "Are you lonely? Do you ever feel alone in your ministry?"

I was taken aback by his directness, but as I recovered I realized I had two options. I could pretend I wasn't lonely (as I had for years—"How could I be lonely," I would ask myself, "when thousands of people know me?") Or I could answer with authenticity and vulnerability.

I heard myself respond, "Yes, at times I do feel alone. I'm surrounded by people, but I'm always in the role of pastor, leader, or manager. Sometimes I need to be just Tim."

Because of Rick's courage, we now meet to deal with our macho tendency to take on the world by ourselves. I suppose women can be macho, too, but maybe we should call it "macha!" Sometimes the pretending isolates us. "Therefore each of you must put off falsehood and speak truthfully to his neighbor, for we are all members of one body" (Ephesians 4:25).

3. Laziness

Youth work can be a haven for lazy people. Whether you're a volunteer or a full-time youth pastor, your work with students can be easy and relatively painless. I think youth ministry attracts lazy people. Where else can you claim to be a "professional" while you wear shorts or jeans every day and get paid to go waterskiing or on fun adventures? Sure, there's a lot of behind-the-scenes work—buying hot dogs, selecting sunscreen, and planning the recreation, for example. But there also is a lot of unaccounted time that can easily be spent on things that don't impact the kingdom of Christ. I know youth pastors who spend hours each day memorizing the sports pages so they can relate to the jocks in their group. I wonder if they have spent much time in the Bible—memorizing the "box scores" of the eternal conquest.

I may sound critical here, and I'll admit my bias. I'm tired of our profession being relegated to the minor leagues of ministry status because youth pastors are perceived to be lazy or incompetent. I'm not sure if it's a perception problem or a performance problem. But I get upset when people say, "When you grow up and become a *real* pastor…" They must have some flaky, lazy, immature youth pastor in mind.

I'm not advocating becoming a workaholic, but some of us could use a little more compulsion for work. We have only so many opportunities to impact young people for Christ. We need to maximize the opportunities God has given us—whether we're volunteers or full-time youth workers. We need to invest our available ministry time wisely. "Be very careful, then, how you live—not as unwise but as wise, making the most of every opportunity, because the days are evil" (Ephesians 5:15-16).

4. Lust

In youth ministry we talk to our students about lust, but we don't talk about *our* lust. We'll get together to talk about friends who have fallen in sexual sin, but we'll avoid sharing our own precarious struggles with sexual temptation. Maybe it's considered a taboo topic for youth workers or, I suppose, Christians in general. It seems inconsistent to talk with teenagers about premarital sex and personal purity but have no dialogue with other youth workers about our own sexuality. Lust gains a foothold in our lives when we pretend we're exempt from it. The denial gives lust power. Bringing it into light can cause it to wither, shrink, and lose its grasp on us.

Youth work can be a very sensual experience. Hormones are raging through the bodies of adolescents who are fascinated with their newly discovered sexuality. Many of them can't wait to try out their "new equipment." Our youth may see us as adults who have become comfortable with our own sexuality. We have weathered the hormonal hurricanes of adolescence and settled into being women and men. A person who is comfortable with his or her sexuality can be very attractive to a teenager. You may be the most attractive model of a male or female to a student in your group. That may fuel your ego—but it also can fuel your folly. Teenagers can become manipulative, seductive, and destructive with their sexuality. Some teenagers have been victimized by the lust of others and live with the shame and pain. As their youth workers, we need to model healthy, pure sexuality. We can be authentic about sexual attraction, but we need to help teenagers discover escape routes from lust. The best way to help our youth deal with lust is to model victory in our own lives.

I define lust as

Living

Under

Sexual

Tension.

Lust is a willful choice that allows natural sexual attraction to get a grip on us and place us under sexual tension. Our focus is influenced by our lust. A youth group can be a dangerous place for a youth worker given to lust. But there is help for those of us who struggle with lust.

"So, if you think you are standing firm, be careful that you don't fall! No temptation has seized you except what is common to man. And God is faithful; he will not let you be tempted beyond what you can bear. But when you are tempted, he will also provide a way out so that you can stand up under it" (I Corinthians 10:12-13).

5. **L**oser mentality

Feeling like a loser can cause a youth worker to lose his or her balance. This feeling shows up in two extremes: "I can't do anything" and "I can do everything." Both imbalances are dangerous. The "I can't" youth worker won't take the risks inherent to youth work. Fearing failure and rejection, the person will play it safe—right down the mediocre middle. The teenagers won't be impressed; they won't be challenged; and they won't remember their youth worker or the things he or she tried to teach.

The "I can" youth worker might be remembered but probably won't last long; this person will burn out early because he or she tried to do it all alone. We need to realize that this kind of unrealistic confidence is often a mask for personal insecurity. These "I can" youth workers are often called "a flash in the pan."

The loss of ego balance can be disastrous for youth workers. If we think we're worthless, we may feel we have nothing to offer the youth. If we think we're God's gift to the youth group, our arrogance may alienate the youth we're supposed to serve.

One place you'll see a lot of strutting and masquerading is at youth worker conferences. Comparison and "group envy" surface quickly as youth workers compare the sizes of their groups and budgets. The youth worker on stage, spotlighted as the one who is really "making it happen," may turn out to be next year's moral tragedy. I don't want to sound judgmental or harsh, but I have noticed a connection between pride and moral failure.

Super Stan

I was interviewing for a job at a church that had a growing reputation for being innovative and culturally relevant. After several applicants from all over the country were considered, the choice came down to me and a youth pastor who lived fifteen hundred miles from the church. I knew the church and the area and was interested in the possibility of going there, but I didn't get the job. They offered it to the other guy.

The pastor told me they selected him because of his impressive accomplishments, national caliber, huge youth group, and dazzling denominational references. I was disappointed with the rejection and began to feel like a loser. I thought I could do the job, and I thought I interviewed well (all six interviews!). They told me I really understood their unique setting, but they chose the other guy! Why? I reflected on the reasons the pastor gave me and concluded that the decision was based on different criteria than what they told me. They changed the rules in the middle of the game! Instead of looking for someone who could lead a balanced and effective youth ministry, they hired a "big shot"—someone with a more impressive pedigree.

Now I was mad as well as sad. I felt the church had compromised its standards. It bugged me so much that I called the pastor back and asked him to explain it to me again. "We chose Stan because of his ability to rally great numbers of students and organize big events," explained the pastor. I hung up feeling like a big loser.

About a year later, the church fired Stan for immorality. Turns out he was lacking integrity sexually *and* ethically. The grand accomplishments listed on his resume turned out to be grossly exaggerated. Some of the references were fabricated. I mourned for the pain and confusion of that youth group. I could picture eyes mutely expressing the pain in hearts hardened by disbelief and cynicism in the wake of this announcement.

My grief was deeper than the rejection I felt. Not getting the job made *me* feel like a loser; betrayal makes *everyone* feel like a loser. I learned a lesson from Stan. A lofty sense of self makes a precarious perch. Or as the Bible says, "Pride goes before destruction, a haughty spirit before a fall" (Proverbs 16:18). Stan felt so low about himself that he had to create a Super Stan. The fantasy may have gotten him the job, but it set him up for destruction.

Our self-esteem needs to be shaped by who we are in Christ, not by our accomplishments. It's Christ's work on the cross that makes the difference, not our works. We really can't discover ourselves until we find ourselves in Jesus. It's his reputation we need to be concerned with, not ours. Being made in the likeness of Christ means our identity is being shaped by Christ, not by our personal ambition or agenda. It basically means letting go of the dying, temporary props for worth and embracing the living, eternal truths that shape us into little imitations of Jesus. "For to me, to live is Christ, and to die is gain" (Philippians 1:21).

A friend of mine had a successful, long-term ministry at a large church and a reputation for helping people discover their spiritual gifts and maximize them in ministry. A larger, prestigious church in another state recruited him to be on staff. He was impressed with the large, modern facilities; the ample budget; the large staff; and the wealthy, well-educated congregation. He took the position but only stayed a matter of months.

When I asked him what happened, he said, "They appealed to my pride. I didn't trust my gut feeling (which was negative). My pride got in the way of making a good decision."

As I listened to him, I made a mental note: "Don't let your pride make your decisions."

6. Last to have my needs met

This is the sixth "L" that can ruin a youth worker. Youth ministry is very demanding. There is no end to the needs we're surrounded by. I'm not sure why you went into youth work. I think a lot of us want to rescue people. We gain a sense of meaning and significance by helping youth, but it's a fine line between compassionate youth worker and co-dependent enabler.

Rescuing a person from the natural consequences of his or her behavior enables that person to continue in irresponsible behavior. Today we call a person who continually rescues another person a co-dependent. In effect, co-dependent, boundaryless people "sign the note" of life for irresponsible people. Then they end up paying the bills—physically, emotionally, and spiritually—and the spendthrifts continue out of control with no consequences. They continue to be loved, pampered, and treated nicely. Favors and sacrifices may be part of the Christian life, but enabling isn't. Learn to tell the difference by evaluating whether your giving is helping the other person become better or worse. The Bible requires responsible action out of the one help is given to. If you don't see it after a season, set limits (Luke 13:9).[7]

Youth workers find it easy to do too much. Attempting to be a mentor, the youth worker may not realize he or she has become a caretaker, encouraging the expectation that "No matter what the problem, you, as my loving youth worker, will take care of me." Sometimes, the most loving thing a youth worker can do is let a teenager experience consequences.

Don't play the role of Rescue Ranger with your teenagers. It may make you feel important, but it can make them dependent and resentful. It can also wear you down.

Devon was one of the most popular youth workers I have known. The kids in our youth group followed him around as if he were the Pied Piper. Devon was single, with a cool apartment near the beach. He often would have a small group of teenagers over for dinner and a game of beach volleyball as the sun set. Devon spent almost all of his free time with adolescents—they were his friends. He was there when Nick had his bout with crack; he helped Sally with her depression. Carol always will remember Devon's persistent care as she struggled with bulimia. Jimmy appreciated Devon's help in talking to his friends about their need for Christ. Wherever there was a need, Devon was there to meet it.

I'll never forget that breakfast with Devon when I stared into his blank, weary eyes. He wasn't his enthusiastic self. Normally he was positive and energetic. This day, his empty gaze was a window to his soul. He was on E, completely drained and emotionally out of gas.

I said, "Devon, you've given so much, there's nothing left for you. You were the last to have your needs met. It's time that Devon took care of Devon."

He broke his fixed, glassy gaze and smiled, "I'm totally burned out, with nothing left to give, and I did it to myself. I'm such a dope—I should know better."

Devon took a sabbatical from youth work. He focused on the personal issues that made him a Rescue Ranger. Through Christian counseling, supportive friends, and accountability, Devon recovered his perspective, balance, and strength. He's back in youth work, but now he can say "no."

Endnotes

1. Tim Kimmel, *Little House on the Freeway* (Portland, OR: Multnomah Press, 1987), 30.

2. Paul Borthwick, *Feeding Your Forgotten Soul: Spiritual Growth for Youth Workers* (Grand Rapids, MI: Zondervan Publishing House, 1990), 105-106.

3. John Ortberg, *The Life You've Always Wanted* (Grand Rapids, MI: Zondervan Publishing House, 1997), 88.

4. Dewey Bertolini, *Back to the Heart of Youthwork* (Wheaton, IL: Victor Books, 1989), 146.

5. Gordon MacDonald, *Renewing Your Spiritual Passion* (Nashville, TN: Oliver Nelson, 1989), 186.

6. Borthwick, *Feeding Your Forgotten Soul: Spiritual Growth for Youth Workers,* 167.

7. Henry Cloud and John Townsend, *Boundaries* (Grand Rapids, MI: Zondervan Publishing House, 1992), 85, 197.

GROUP DISCUSSION QUESTIONS
Chapter 6: *The Balancing Act*
Nurture Your Soul With Balance

1. What do you think you would notice if you returned to our culture after being in a third world country for a year? Explain.

2. In *Little House on the Freeway*, Tim Kimmel says our society values being hurried and we have a love affair with haste. How do you relate to his statements personally and in your youth ministry?

3. Which of the four balancing acts do you find the hardest? Why?

   Personal time versus ministry time

   Thought time versus activity time

   Time with adults versus time with students

   Time with parents versus time with students

4. Review the myths that lead to imbalance (pp. 81-84). What parts of them seem true? What parts are dangerously false?

5. Evaluate your personal ministry balance by using the Time Pinwheel on page 86. Shade the pie slices according to how much time you spend on that piece. Share and discuss your pinwheels.

6. Which of the six common L vices of youth workers do you think is most destructive? Why?

7. What are some ideas to use to counter these destructive habits?

The Big Adventure

CHAPTER 7
The Big Adventure

Nurture Your Soul With Risk

Jesus challenges us with a call to adventure. He didn't say, "Take up your couch and follow me." He said, "Take up your cross and follow me." He didn't promise miracles, an influential position, or wealth. He offered the unknown. When Christ calls people, he doesn't offer a ten-year growth plan with benefits. He says, "Follow me." When Christ calls, he calls us from a life of comfort and certainty to a journey through challenge and uncertainty. A journey of faith involves risk. We have chosen to follow Christ, not because he has told us the details of what lies ahead on the journey, but because we believe in him and trust his leadership. When Christ says, "Follow me," he's asking us if we're willing to have an intimate relationship with him, an adventure with him as our guide.

Effective youth workers understand that life can be the greatest adventure of all if we have the right guide. Their goal is to introduce youth to the guide and get them excited about the adventure of the faith journey. Seeing life as an adventure requires a willingness to take risks: to try new things, to experience the unfamiliar, and to travel with people who force us to grow. Embarking on the adventure requires a willingness to risk leaving comfort zones behind.

For me, it meant going to Eastern Europe right after the 1989 revolution that ended the dictatorship of Nicolai Ceausescu in Romania.

Ministry on the Orient Express

Twenty-one youth workers from the United States descended on Eastern Europe with the idea of training Eastern European youth workers in basic principles of youth ministry. To pull this off, we all had to travel on the infamous Orient Express. I hadn't even been on the train, and I was spooked. But the train from Vienna was sleek, modern, and aluminum. The ride was pleasant and quick, and it emanated Austrian efficiency.

This Eastern Europe stuff ain't so bad, I thought as I waited on the platform for the next train. Then a sudden clanging and creaking caught my attention. I saw a brown wood crate on wheels. It looked like a boxcar with windows. People gazed expressionlessly through the grimy windows. As they stepped off the train, I noticed that they were uniformly dressed in black, brown, or gray.

Five of us piled into a taxi the size of a Yugo, and we sped off to the hotel. Traffic was horrendous, but it didn't bother the cabby. He simply swerved onto the cable car track and passed all the cars, playing chicken with the cable car. To avoid certain death, he veered back into traffic and screeched to a skidding stop in the middle of an intersection, against the light! I had been in Eastern Europe only minutes, and my life was flashing before my eyes.

Why am I here? Why didn't I stay in sunny Southern California? Then I remembered that we were here on a mission. Yeah, that's it—"a mission from God." Well, at least *for* God. We wanted to encourage and train the youth workers in Eastern Europe. For years, they had had to do everything in secret. Now they had a little more freedom, and we wanted to act in this window of opportunity.

At the hotel we enjoyed a delicious meal and talked about why we were there. Believers from Romania, Hungary, Czechoslovakia, and Poland had asked

Western missionaries to send youth workers to train their people. Reach Out Ministries, under the direction of Barry St. Clair, was asked to coordinate this trip. Our contact, John Howard, was a full-time missionary.

As we stuffed ourselves, we each wondered what our trip would be like. After this meal we would separate into teams and head off to our destinations. "Will we get lost?" "Will we be able to find our contact?" "Will the KGB or *Securitate* trail us?" "Should we be using the 'Cone of Silence' as we talk?" Excitement, fear, and wonder filled the air.

Later, at 1 a.m., we pulled ourselves off the cold cement floor of the cavernous train station and walked past hundreds of fellow travelers and homeless people, most of them asleep amid their meager possessions, stepping carefully to avoid the pools of slush and urine. The Orient Express waited for us, belching toxic smoke and quivering in the freezing December night. We boarded the wooden boxcar and squeezed down the smoke-filled, twenty-four-inch-wide hallway, bumping almost every one of the people crammed into standing-room-only positions.

I maneuvered my way to my berth and quickly fell asleep. A few hours later, I was shaken awake by the lurching of the Orient Express as it screeched to a halt. The conductor shouted the name of the stop, and Barry and his team prepared to unload their baggage onto the platform of this obscure Romanian railroad depot. The conductor warned them that the train stopped for only a few minutes and they would have to hurry.

I poked my head out the window to say "goodbye"—I was too cozy in my berth to leave it—and saw a picture of speed and agility degenerate into one of confusion, clumsiness, and sheer terror. Barry and his team had deftly unloaded all their stuff, only to realize they were at the wrong station! As the train pulled away, they tried desperately to get their baggage back into it.

Barry St. Clair's signature outfit is a warm-up suit, and he was wearing one that day as he chased a train on the snowy plains of rural Romania. In an imitation of those movie scenes where the hero is chasing the train and leaps to catch it, Barry dove for the train, only to fall flat on his face on the platform. A look of disgust, failure, and fear filled his face. The team had managed to get most of their baggage and one of the team members on the train. But three of the team members where stranded at the wrong depot. None of them spoke Romanian.

We hailed the conductor and were told that the next stop was the right one, but the conductor warned us about the gypsies who attack people and steal their possessions. I'll never forget the next stop. We left Mike alone, sitting on twelve bags of stuff, at 5:30 in the cold Romanian morning. As we pulled out, I noticed a large group of gypsies staring at Mike and laughing.

I thought, "So this is what it means to be a martyr."

That morning, and at every other uncertain turn of our adventure, God was gracious and rescued us from peril. Barry's team soon was reunited, and Mike spent the morning chatting with gypsies, telling them about God and why he'd come to Romania. I'm sure they couldn't figure out why he'd brought so much stuff.

Brasov, Romania

We arrived at the Brasov depot, unloaded our luggage, and tried to maintain a low profile until our contact arrived. Three youth workers trying to blend in with Romanian travelers is like Michael Jordan trying to blend in at a Shriners convention. It just doesn't work! We were wearing dark clothes and the right shoes, and we weren't talking, but dozens of people stared at us. I felt like I was wearing a neon sign flashing, "Secret Police, look here! An American!"

A woman spotted us and immediately came over and asked in heavily accented English, "You are Americans, no?"

"Yes, we are," I said hesitantly, wanting to make sure she wasn't *Securitate*.

"You are here to help young people, yes?"

"Yes, we are," answered Jamie with his Tennessee accent.

"You know Shohn Hovard, yes?" she tested us with the code.

"Yes, we are with Reach Out Ministries," answered Bruce.

We introduced ourselves to the young woman, Dori, who then said, "We go now!"

I responded, "If you'd like to take us to the hotel, that would be fine."

"No, no, you stay with us," Dori replied.

"No, really, we don't want to be a burden to you," explained Bruce.

"Bruce Lee!" exclaimed Dori (she had seen the movies), "In Brasov I am boss!" Her sense of humor and brashness were a welcome surprise on this venture. We had encountered one strong woman. You have to be strong to be in youth ministry, especially in Romania.

When Adam, Dori's husband, returned from his job at the factory, we prepared for the training of youth workers at his church. Adam had successfully pulled together a covert network of twenty-four youth workers and hundreds of youth. To avoid detection by the *Securitate*, they would have their rallies in the forest. People would come from different directions, at different times, to avoid arousing suspicion. Our training session would be the first time youth workers had met openly in a church to discuss youth ministry in over forty years!

Youth workers came from all over Transylvania to attend this training. They were nervous because this was so new and excited because we all sensed the beginning of something bigger than all of us.

"It is a blessing from God to see all of us in one room. Never before has this happened," said Cornel, the youth worker from the Pentecostal church.

"I never dreamed I'd see the day when we would share fellowship openly with other youth workers, let alone our brothers from the west," said Emil with moist eyes.

Romania was an entire country off-balance, uncertain, confused, and tense. The church as an organization reflected this insecurity, but, as individuals, most Romanian believers thought deeper, prayed with more sincerity, lived more sacrificially, evaluated more consistently, and laughed more boisterously than Westerners. They lived valued lives. They understood the risk of the faith journey.

That night sixty-seven students came to the *Explosia Bucureia* (Joy Explosion), five of them committing their lives to Jesus. The youth workers were elated. Not only had they received training in evangelism and discipleship, but revival was breaking out in Brasov, a city previously known for its recent revolutionary martyrs.

"We now can celebrate the blood of Christ in Brasov, not simply the blood of brothers and sisters!" exclaimed Daniel, the youth worker from the Second Baptist Church.

The night before we left Brasov, we exchanged gifts with our hosts. Dori handed me a wrapped gift, smiling sheepishly. Inside I found a beautiful handwoven sweater with artistic patterns native to that area of Romania.

"It's for Brooke, your little daughter," Dori said.

I was astonished. Dori had followed me around the store that day, noting what sweaters I liked, and secretly purchased one for Brooke. The emotion of the moment was overwhelming. Her generosity was compelling. The sweater was expensive by Romanian standards, about four days' wages!

I was reminded of 2 Corinthians 8:2-4: "Out of the most severe trial their overflowing joy and their extreme poverty welled up in rich generosity. For I testify that they gave as much as they were able, and even beyond their ability. Entirely on their own, they urgently pleaded with us for the privilege of sharing in this service to the saints."

It was that winter in Romania when I learned about the reality and depth of the abundant life. "The thief comes only to steal and kill and destroy; I have come that they may have life, and have it to the full" (John 10:10).

My Romanian friends evidenced a rare, internal strength and vitality. I saw in them the principle-centered people Stephen Covey described.

"Principle-centered people savor life. Because their security comes from within instead of from without, they have no need to categorize and stereotype everything and everybody in life to give them a sense of certainty and predictability. They see old faces freshly, old scenes as if for the first time. They're like courageous explorers going on an expedition into uncharted territories; they really aren't sure what's going to happen, but they're confident it will be exciting and growth producing and they will discover new territory and make new contributions. Their security lies in their initiative, resourcefulness, creativity, willpower, courage, stamina, and native intelligence rather than in the safety, protection, and abundance of their home camps, of their comfort zones.

"They rediscover people each time they meet them. They are interested in them. They ask questions and get involved. They are completely present when they listen. They learn from them. They don't label them from past successes or failures. They see no one bigger than life. They are not overawed by top government figures or celebrities. They resist becoming any person's disciple. They are basically unflappable and capable of adapting to virtually anything that comes along. One of their fixed principles is flexibility. They truly lead the abundant life."[1]

My Romanian friends had seen the ravages of the thief who sought to destroy them, but they were more alive and more committed to living a life on the cutting edge than ever. They understood that living a life of faith means taking risks. It means doing the right thing and living with the consequences. Faith is trusting God more than we trust our own personal protective skills. I came back from Romania a changed man. I began to see that I needed to challenge my youth group in the big adventure. I wanted them to capture the excitement of what God is doing throughout the world. There is much to be enthusiastic about. The key is discovering what God is doing and joining him in it. God's plans will be made real with us or without us, but I want the adventure of being involved with what God is doing.

As I was sharing my adventure with a group, someone in the back said, "How can you be positive about what's going on? Aren't things getting worse over there and in the world all over?"

"Yes," I replied, "Some things are getting worse. The kingdom of darkness is growing, but so is the kingdom of light! And I'm rejoicing because I know which kingdom wins in the end!"

Rivers or Reservoirs?

Christ has given us living water; we can choose to soak it up like a giant sponge and keep it to ourselves—to be a reservoir. Or we can choose to be a channel of God's benefits to others—and be a river. Every day we make choices, large and small, that reveal which we're becoming—rivers or reservoirs. Rivers are mighty and powerful, and people are captivated by their grandeur. Reservoirs are forgettable and boring; they're too self-serving. Youth groups (like youth workers) can be either.

The more churches give away blessings, the more they are likely to be blessed. These churches are focused on others rather than themselves, open to outsiders with their new ideas and ways, and inclusive rather than exclusive. They're outreaching rather than self-fortifying, an army of lifesavers rather than a club of those once saved. These are the churches of the twenty-first century. A basic principle for church growth says, "For a church to grow, it must want to grow and be willing to pay the price." The price is counted least in dollars. It's paid in the more costly currency of change. It's doing church in new ways, incorporating new people, moving out of comfort zones, and existing for others rather than for self. [2]

Dynamic youth workers understand the adventure that comes with seeing needs and taking the risk of meeting them. They know they probably won't be able to meet all the needs, but they will meet some. They may be criticized for seeking to be relevant, but they're more concerned with reaching those people who need the gospel than with listening to the complaints of those already saturated with the gospel.

For reasons I can't fathom, some believers seem to feel a sense of scarcity when reaching out, as if they had limited resources. They act as if we need to keep these good things to ourselves, as if we might lose something if we let too many people in on it! I can't imagine anything further from Christ's great commission (Matthew 28:19-20).

Mature believers see life from an abundance paradigm—they see that there is plenty of grace to go around. There is enough good news for the whole world! The goal of those who feel a sense of abundance is to help as many people as possible to understand that Jesus offers us life at its maximum potential. They're enthusiastic because they see life as an adventure that God empowers them to pursue.

How do you view life? There are three ways to walk through life:

• Are you a **traveler**—one who just wants to get through the trip and reach the destination? Are you simply enduring this life until you get to heaven?

• Are you a **tourist**—one who stops by the side of the road at "Scenic View" signs, pulls out a camera, and snaps a shot of the scenery?

• Or are you an **explorer**—one who veers off the road most traveled and pursues adventure by hiking to the scenic places? We can make our life journey an adventure if we begin to see ourselves as explorers—people who dare to go beyond the comfort of cars or easy chairs. Effective youth workers don't appeal to tradition or comfort, but to community and the common cause of living out the big adventure.

The Risk of Change

Most of us want to be like Christ. But we want the transformation to be on the fast track. We want none of this slow, persevering, suffering kind of spiritual metamorphosis. *Can't God just zap us with his magic wand?*

We have settled for a mediocre view of spiritual transformation. We want just a little bit of God. We don't want so much that we'll become weird or extreme, just enough to improve ourselves. We have settled for a cosmetic transformation.

What would happen if we really risked it? I mean, if we bet the farm? What would happen if we really did put it all on the line for Christ? What would happen to you and your youth group if you didn't settle for cosmetic transformation? if instead of talking about love, you started loving? if instead of taking a stand for righteousness and against sin, you sat with a sinner and listened?

I've noticed that sometimes I put more effort into acting like a loving person than I do actually loving others. And I strive to make a demonstrative stand for what's right and wonder why others aren't as virtuous as I am.

These actions are evidence of cosmetic transformation. They indicate that the change in me didn't get to the root of the problem. It's like trying to improve the appearance of my yard by chopping off the tops of the dandelions. The grass might look good for a day, but I really didn't solve the problem.

Genuine transformation doesn't settle for cosmetic changes. It goes for the root. When we're open to transformational growth, we won't throw up smoke screens of external touch-up. We'll take the risk of being totally changed.

"The misunderstanding of true spirituality has caused immense damage to the human race. Tragically, it's possible to think we're becoming more spiritual when in fact we're becoming only more smug and judgmental. Pseudo-transformation means becoming what Mark Twain once called 'a good man in the worst sense of the word.'" [3]

Our youth are looking for authenticity. They're also looking for adventure. We can offer them both as we model a life of genuine transformation—a life that risks letting God shape us into the image of Jesus.

Be an explorer, take the risk of radical abandon to Jesus Christ. As you walk with him, you'll pick up some of his qualities.

Our youth groups are full of postmodern students who are looking for authenticity and adventure. As Dave Urbanski wrote in his article, "Perspectives on the Next Generation," "Modernism basically says you can believe what you want, as long as it doesn't make any difference in the way you live. But postmodernism says that convictions and practices cannot be separated. Rodney Clapp said, 'Christians can no longer say, "Don't look at us; look at Jesus." We are the Body of Christ! We are how God has chosen to make Jesus present. Therefore faith must no longer be an abstract certainty, but an embodied confidence.'" [4]

Endnotes

1. Stephen R. Covey, *Principle-Centered Leadership* (New York: Simon & Schuster, Inc., 1992), 37.

2. Leith Anderson, *A Church for the 21st Century* (Minneapolis, MN: Bethany House Publishers, 1992), 192.

3. John Ortberg, *The Life You've Always Wanted,* (Grand Rapids, MI: Zondervan Publishing House, 1997), 38.

4. Dave Urbanski, "Perspectives on the Next Generation," Youthworker (January/February 1999), 31.

GROUP DISCUSSION QUESTIONS
Chapter 7: *The Big Adventure*
Nurture Your Soul With Risk

1. Have you ever gone on an adventure that has changed your life? Describe what happened.

2. Why do you think the Romanian believers think deeper, pray with more sincerity, live more sacrificially, evaluate more consistently, and laugh more boisterously than Westerners?

3. What do you think Jesus meant when he said, "I have come that they may have life, and have it to the full"?

4. Who has been a river of living water in your life? What is it about that person that makes him or her distinctive?

5. What do you think about the three ways to journey through life (p. 103)? Do you identify with the traveler, the tourist, or the explorer? Explain.

6. Brainstorm some ways you could become more of an explorer.

Chapter 8
Collective Soul

Nurture Your Soul Through Community

I was headed to the High Sierras with several guys from my youth group, but, after six hours of driving and a horrendous traffic jam in Los Angeles, I was exhausted.

"I'll be glad to drive," offered Steve.

I was reluctant to let him drive, but he was eighteen and insured.

"OK," I said. "But wake me up if you have any problems."

Steve said he would. Then he asked, "How do I get to Mammoth?"

"Just stay on this freeway until you get to 395 and take it north," I told him. I crawled in the back of the van and swiftly went to sleep.

After about two hours, I awakened with a strange feeling. Everyone was asleep except Steve, who was drumming his fingers on the steering wheel to the beat blasting from the stereo. I glanced at the speedometer under his pulsating digits. Eighty miles per hour! Steve was speeding!

Then I noticed something just ahead on the freeway. Less than a few miles away, a gigantic bubble of light interrupted the navy blue blankness of the desert night.

"Vegas!" I yelled at Steve, a fusion of anger and worry adding volume to my voice. "You're driving us at eighty miles per hour to Las Vegas!" My words woke up the other campers.

"Wow! We're going to Vegas. Cool!" growled Robert.

"You were supposed to turn on 395!" I lectured.

"I never saw it. This way's fine. We'll just find a way to go from here," explained Steve.

"It's too far from here—we're way out of the way," I whined.

"You can't get there from here," joked Lance.

"We'll have to go through Death Valley. It'll take us all night," I whimpered.

"Yeah, but look what great progress we're making. I've been going eighty to ninety miles per hour for over two hours. Who cares if we're lost—we're making good time!" exclaimed Steve with a totally straight face.

To this day, I reflect on this episode as an illustration of classic ineffectiveness. "Who cares if we're lost, we're making good time!" A variation on this theme is, "Who cares if we're doing the wrong thing, we're *doing* it right, aren't we?" Another analogy is reaching the top rung of the ladder of success, only to find it leaning against the wrong building.

If we're going to be effective leaders, we need to have a broader focus than methods or efficiency. As Peter Drucker says, "Efficiency is doing things right. Effectiveness is doing the right things." One of the right things is building a team.

In *Principle-Centered Leadership*, Stephen Covey describes the need for an "effectiveness-minded approach to leadership." He writes, "A strategic leader can provide direction and vision, motivate through love, and build a complementary team based on mutual respect if he is more effectiveness-minded than efficiency-minded, more concerned with direction and results than with methods, systems, and procedures."[1]

We were making good time on that freeway, but it was in the wrong direction. If we evaluate our progress in youth work by how far we've come, we need to make sure we're going in the right direction.

A Vacuum of Leadership

In his discussion of leadership, Covey discusses the differences between three roles that are essential to all organizations: producer, manager, and leader.[2]

Each of these roles is "vital to the success of the organization," but each is distinct and different. Producers are the ones who act on new ideas and create products. Managers coordinate the work and the workers. Leaders provide the vision and direction for the team. Without the leader, people "perish" because there is no vision. Strategic leadership is crucial for the continued success of any team.

"Leadership deals with direction—with making sure the ladder is leaning against the right wall. Management deals with speed. To double one's speed in the wrong direction, however, is the very definition of foolishness. Leadership deals with vision—with keeping the mission in sight—and with effectiveness and results. Management deals with establishing structure and systems to get those results. It focuses on efficiency, cost-benefit analyses, logistics, methods, procedures, and policies.

"Leadership focuses on the top line. Management focuses on the bottom line. Leadership derives its power from values and correct principles. Management organizes resources to serve selected objectives to produce the bottom line."[3]

Effective leaders are team builders; they acknowledge that performing at peak levels requires the cooperation and contribution of each teammate. The leader's challenge is to minimize the distraction and the tension on the team. Individual differences can be affirmed; we all have our strengths and our roles to play. Mutual appreciation and respect create an environment for a competent and complementary team—one where the strength lies in differences.

"The body is a unit, though it is made up of many parts; and though all its parts are many, they form one body. So it is with Christ…If the whole body were an eye, where would the sense of hearing be? If the whole body were an ear, where would the sense of smell be? But in fact God has arranged the parts in the body, every one of them, just as he wanted them to be. If they were all one part, where would the body be? As it is, there are many parts, but one body" (1 Corinthians 12:12, 17-20).

Each part of the body of Christ is meaningful and offers something beneficial to the whole. It would be a disservice to the body to try to make each part function in the same way. It would be ineffective, and the effort would devalue the individuality and giftedness of each part.

In effective teams of youth workers, too, each person needs to be valued for his or her individual worth and contribution. People's "differentness" needs to be celebrated rather than minimized. The goal is to make each strength more productive and each weakness less relevant. The focus is on contribution, affirmation, and appreciation.

The first step in building genuine community is building a team spirit among the adult volunteers. When the leaders model community, the students will follow their example.

However, building genuine community requires a paradigm shift. It would involve at least these five changes:

• *from program to people*

Our focus needs to shift from the needs of our program to the needs of the people. If we're going to build an effective team, we need to be concerned with the needs of the team players, as well as the needs of the targeted ministry people. This change in focus has implications for how we recruit people for our youth worker teams. If we switch our paradigm from program to people, we won't recruit people for positions for which they aren't gifted or called to. In other words, we won't manipulate a person to fill a position.

• *from production to principles*

Instead of concentrating on the production of a program, we'll pursue principle-driven ministry. The difference between production and principles was discussed in Chapter 5. Here we're developing the idea that it's easier to build a team around the concept of building principles into team members' lives than it is to simply build toward a production. Principle-driven ministry offers a solid foundation for effective teams. People can feel used if all they do is contribute to something flashy but short-lived. In contrast, joining with others in committing to a cause often leads to personal growth and a feeling of value. Production and principle sometimes look very much alike. The difference is that production is looking for the short-term pay off, and principle-oriented ministry focuses on long-term growth.

• *from past to future*

Team building requires a future-focused perspective. We can't afford the luxury of looking at life through the rear view mirror. People are interested in joining a team that has a future, not simply a "blast from the past!"

One of the saddest interviews I've had was with a historic church with a rich evangelical tradition. Church leaders showed me pictures of their historic church in its heyday and dropped names from the "Who's Who" of the church's past. Then they asked me if I wanted to "join their team." I felt like I was being recruited to go live in a mausoleum! All the heroes were dead, the staff lived in their shadows, and there was no vision for the future. It's difficult to be motivated to join a team that has a past but no future. I turned down the job. I'd rather sign on with a team that has a promising future than be part of one with a notable past. People are more committed to shaping the future than preserving the past.

• *from obstacles to opportunities*

People love to be around winners. It's the winner's locker room that's crowded after the big game, while the loser's locker room is quiet and reflective. In the game of life, we see people who always seem to be winners—even in the midst of adversity. They know how to turn every obstacle into an opportunity and every failure into a lesson.

A team with this attitude can be technically mediocre and still have a decided advantage. Why? Because this positive, what-can-we-learn-from-this mentality keeps people in an open and learning frame of mind. People who are teachable are more capable because they receive additional input that will help them transform every obstacle into an opportunity.

• *from fear of criticism to cultural relevance*

Fear can be a very strong motivator. In building an effective team, though, it's important to minimize the influence of fear. The best way to make fear unimportant may be to acknowledge its influence. If we're to bring out the best in team members, we need to address their fears, accept and affirm them as valid, and then gently point the team members toward the fears and needs of others. People often gain a feeling of control and renewed courage when they realize they aren't alone with their fears. Team members must be willing to look at each other and say, "I'm afraid this might not work" and feel supported with that fear.

However, I'm convinced that many ministries are destined to ineffectiveness because they're motivated by fear.

Think about how many times someone has come up with a creative idea in response to a specific need in the community only to have the idea quenched by a comment such as, "That's a great idea, but it would really raise questions from some of the deacons," or "Wouldn't that be seen as worldly or compromising?" Leaders who think they're being spiritual and sensitive (politically correct) may be making decisions based on fear.

Jesus focused on meeting needs regardless of the social fallout. In an awkward moment at dinner, an uninvited female with a dubious reputation crashed the party and, with great passion, kissed Christ's feet. As her tears bathed his feet, she wiped them with her hair. The religious big shots of the day commented on Jesus' lack of discernment and discretion. "If this man were a prophet, he would know who is touching him and what kind of woman she is—that she is a sinner" (Luke 7:39).

Christ didn't respond to this criticism. Instead, he ignored the Pharisees and utilized the teachable moment to tell Simon a story about forgiveness. This is the right perspective: to remember always that we have been forgiven much.

We shouldn't be critical of others; we should see them as fellow sinners in need of grace. Another lesson we might learn from this parable is that we don't need to allow critical religious people to keep us from meeting the needs of secular folks.

Christ shows us how to be culturally relevant without compromising the lesson. He socialized with sinners—those who pretended they weren't and those who knew they were. He was available to people who needed the gospel. He was on their turf and was relaxed—they were having dinner. His focus was on the needs of people, not *his* need to look socially respectable. In this case, I think he walked the balance by showing respect for the woman's need as he showed respect for the needs of the religious elite. By allowing the woman to continue anointing his feet, Christ set up a situation that would illustrate to the cynical saints their need for true repentance. Christ affirmed both needs for spiritual renewal by being relevant to the sinful woman and the sinful Pharisees. In the midst of all this dramatic tension, Christ didn't compromise the gospel. He kept the focus consistently on sin, forgiveness, and love.

Today, when people suggest that being culturally relevant is an automatic compromise of the gospel, we can point to the example of Christ who showed us that we can be culturally relevant without being ashamed of the gospel.

A Strategy for Synergy

Once we have the paradigm for team building, we need to have a strategy for synergy. "Synergy is the state in which the whole is more important than the sum of the parts" (see Chapter 1). Synergistic youth work seeks to affirm the value and contribution of each individual to the team. The youth worker who understands synergy will make students and staff feel valuable by affirming their personal contributions and unique qualities. He or she will show individuals how their contributions and giftedness benefit the whole group. As each person feels valued, affirmed, and meaningful, a spirit of teamwork can develop. Synergy can't be forced. It must be grown. As it grows, it takes on a life of its own. This life is energy produced by the cooperative spirit of people working effectively together.

Successful businessman Max Depree offers some excellent advice. "Effective influencing and understanding spring largely from healthy relationships among the members of the group. Leaders need to foster environments and work processes within which people can develop high-quality relationships—relationships with each other, relationships with the group with which we work, relationships with our clients and customers."[4]

From a Biblical perspective, synergy begins with an understanding of the diversity of spiritual gifts and God-given personalities. As we understand and respect our diversity, we're able to begin trusting each other and learning to value each other. We learn to think in a new way about the strengths of others. We realize we can sing in a key we don't usually sing in and still sound harmonious.

Effective leaders are learners because they're always open to new ways of doing things. They seek to empower people to make decisions on their own and determine their own sphere of influence.

For example, we assign our students to small-group leaders who make their own choices about what they'll do with their groups. The small-group leaders work within basic guidelines, but they also have a lot of freedom to choose. With their students' input, they decide what outside activities the group will do, how to structure the group's time, and the level of accountability and care they want to have as a group. This emphasis on decentralized empowerment and grass-roots decision-making isn't just a business trend, it's a principle that is centuries old.

"There are different kinds of gifts, but the same Spirit. There are different kinds of service, but the same Lord. There are different kinds of working, but the same God works all of them in all men…The body is a unit, though it is made up of many parts; and though all its parts are many, they form one body. So it is with Christ. For we were all baptized by one Spirit into one body—whether Jews or Greeks, slave or free—and we were all given the one Spirit to drink" (1 Corinthians 12:4-6, 12-14).

Effective youth workers understand synergy, and they strive to develop it. They know a team with synergy will recruit for itself because prospective volunteers will want to get in on the action. People are seeking the meaning, encouragement, and community they can experience on a spiritually unified team.

I like what author Alan Loy McGinnis says about team-building. "The leader who can learn the laws of group morale becomes a highly valuable commodity, for not only does good 'esprit de corps' enable people to get the job done in half the time, it also draws in new people. Some of the most successful churches, for instance, are led by pastors who do not have magnetic personalities. Their success is due rather to the skill with which they build an enthusiastic, cohesive congregation. So in such cases people are drawn not so much to the leader but to the group feeling—the high-energy atmosphere. Good leaders set out to do far more than build allegiance to themselves, which is important, of course, but it is not enough. It is also necessary to build into the organization an allegiance to each other."[5]

Enemies of Team Spirit

One of the most destructive synergy-killers is competition. Competition that pits team members against each other instead of their common opponent brings out the worst in a team. As Christians, our enemy is Satan. We need to stand together against him and all that would seek to elevate him and destroy Christian faith. Our primary competition is in the spiritual arena.

Competition destroys synergy when the focus becomes winning. I know of a youth director who organized volleyball games on Sunday afternoons, but few of his youth would attend. The youth director had to be on the winning team; if he wasn't, he'd fume and fuss and stomp off to his office for a pity party. His competitive spirit killed any opportunity for community in that youth group.

There will always be competition in athletics, business, and life. What must change is the intensity that turns competition into combat. A wise youth worker knows how to tame competition with cooperation.

A look at the root meaning of "compete" is revealing—even surprising. The Latin source is "competere," meaning "to come together, agree, be suitable, belong, compete for." Nothing in this original definition of competing suggests the need for a killer instinct. We have added that little feature by coming to believe that excellence can be achieved only at the expense of others.[6]

Many of us are getting fed up with the win-lose, self-centered, look-out-for-number-one "me-ism" that's common in our culture. There has to be a way we can cooperate, even in the midst of some lively competition.

If you have a team member who is so competitive that he or she is hurting the team in an effort to win, share with that person these ideas on competition. Let him or her know that the killer instinct is from the world and not from the Spirit of God. Challenge the team member to fight the fight that is worth fighting. The competitive spirit is often misdirected. "For our struggle is not against flesh and blood, but against the rulers, against the authorities, against the powers of this dark world and against the spiritual forces of evil in the heavenly realms" (Ephesians 6:12).

Let's keep in mind who our real enemy is. We don't need to compete with other youth workers or youth ministries.[7]

Another enemy of team spirit is lack of communication. Everyone on the team should be able to describe in a sentence the purpose of your youth ministry. These descriptions should sound amazingly alike because you have worked on communicating purpose. Once you have developed and articulated your purpose statement, come up with three or four priorities for your youth ministry. Here are some examples:

1. to develop small groups so that every student is assigned to a leader for weekly care and Bible study.

2. to offer events that appeal to non-Christians as well as Christians.

3. to challenge our youth to practice their faith by offering service projects four times a year.

If a youth leader is asked what the group is all about, the leader can share the purpose statement (in his or her own words) and say, "We're working to have each teenager in a small group, to make the youth group a safe place to invite friends from school, and to challenge youth to really live out their faith by serving." This type of common language significantly helps establish community and enhances communication. Communication is key to team spirit.

"Communicate extensively to create the link between causes and the commitment individual employees make to those causes. You can't force people to be committed; neither can you control whether they stay committed. The best approach is to be the source of clear, consistent, honest information. *When in doubt, tell people too much.* The more they know about your cause, the more they can help in ways you wouldn't have expected. The more they find they can help, the more commitment they feel. Respect people enough to be straight with them about the down side as well as the up side; that too, strengthens commitment."[8] (emphasis added)

I like the phrase, "When in doubt, tell people too much." I find that problems arise when I *assume* my team understands. I'm discovering that we have a stronger team if I communicate consistently. I'm trying to communicate until I get the response, "Yes, you've told us that before," coupled with the muttered, "several times you've told us."

That response let's me know I've effectively communicated.

The bottom line is: Don't assume people understand your message. Clearly communicate it several times and in several ways. Building community requires clear communication.

A third enemy of team spirit is *conflict*. There will come a time when team members disagree. Your role as leader is not to ignore the conflict (although ignoring it will work in some cases) but to seek to resolve the conflict. Separate the people from the problem. Extract the personalities and focus on the issue. When people feel they have been heard, they usually choose to move toward reconciliation or compromise.

When resolving conflict, it's important to seek first to understand, rather than to be understood. Make sure you do much listening and little lecturing. An effective team leader tries hard not to lose anyone over a disagreement, but this leader also refuses to allow conflict to destroy the team.

Affirm to both sides that conflict is a natural part of being on a team. It doesn't have to be disastrous as long as team members talk about the issues and play fair. Some of our best lessons can come out of times of conflict. Encourage people to talk directly to the team members they're having trouble with and not to talk to others unnecessarily.

A conflict on our staff resulted in the resignation of a team member who didn't like the way her leader was treating her. I was out of town when the conflict occurred. When I returned, I was told that everything was fine and that it had been dealt with. It wasn't fine. The woman who had quit—let's call her Louise—was really upset about the disrespect demonstrated by "Thelma," her leader.

"She's really into control. She only wanted me to do it her way," Louise said, dabbing tears from her eyes.

"I was told it was dealt with," I inquired.

"Not from my point of view."

"I'm here to listen to your side. I want you to know you're important and a valuable member on our team."

"Thanks. I don't feel very valuable. Especially after how I was treated."

I spent two hours listening to Louise describe the feelings of hurt that resulted from the conflict. I learned that she felt Thelma had treated her abruptly and harshly. As a result, Louise quit our team. My time listening seemed to help her process her hurt. I assured her that there still was a place for her on the team.

I then called Thelma and heard her side of the conflict. Within a few days, we were able to resolve the conflict, but it took work. It also took the courage to not sweep it under the carpet or ignore it.

As Christians, we will have conflict. As mature Christians, we should seek to resolve conflict and learn from it, rather than pretend it doesn't exist.

As Jerry White points out in his book, *Dangers Men Face*, "Jesus instructs us first to be reconciled with our brothers and sisters before offering spiritual sacrifices since we can't have intimate fellowship with God when we're in a state of conflict (Matthew 5:24).

"The result of conflict in a community of believers is disunity and dissension.

This is a sad witness to the nonbelieving world. Conflicts in the Christian family lead to divisions and rifts in relationships that may last for a lifetime. Men and women everywhere are deeply wounded by such conflict."[9]

Of course, some people seem to create conflict. You know those people; they look like they were weaned on a dill pickle. If you have one of these troublemakers who consistently seeks conflict, share with him or her the following verse: "He who loves a quarrel loves sin" (Proverbs 17:19a).

The Effective Team Leader

- has vision

- has character and integrity

- searches out competence

- leads through serving

- communicates easily at all levels

- is approachable and available to others (is a listener)

- is open to contrary opinion

- is committed to fairness and advocates it

- values the contributions, skills, and talents of others, but values the person more than the task

- makes it a priority to be in touch with the organization and its work

- is a spokesperson and diplomat

- is able to see the big picture (beyond his or her own area of focus)

- understands and passes on the stories and culture of the organization

- tells *why* rather than *how*

- can rejoice with those who rejoice and weep with those who weep

- is able to utilize different styles of leadership in different settings and situations

- is committed to a legacy (something that lives beyond him or her)

- is accountable and holds others to accountability

- enables others to realize their full potential as persons

- has earned the respect of others

Putting Together the Dream Team

The kind of people you choose will determine how much synergy you have on your team. Certain qualities make people particularly good candidates for a team of youth workers. In his book *Growing Up Christian,* Jim Marian reminds us of the importance of relating to youth as we seek to disciple them. [10] Three traits that characterize a relational approach to discipling youth are availability, modeling, and accountability.

Availability—We're so busy today that youth have few adults to relate to. Being available is a way we can show teenagers they're important to us. Hanging out with kids helps them believe what we say because they see us putting it into action.

Modeling—Many Christian kids are in the process of throwing away the style of their parents' faith and looking for a faith style that fits them. Providing alternative models for a healthy faith is one important role for a youth worker. I seek to recruit staff who look different, act different, like different music, and relate to kids differently than I do. But they must have in common a growing, passionate love for Christ and a desire to see that love develop in teenagers.

Accountability—In my opinion, all youth workers need to be held accountable to someone. I'm not talking about checking in weekly for what you ate, how often you did your quiet times, or whether you shared your faith. I'm talking about having a mentor or a small group of people who will hold you accountable to grow as a believer. This group could be the youth team itself.

Accountability helps us balance the external with the internal. We can't ask our students to be accountable if we aren't. Groups that exercise some kind of accountability among their leaders tend not to have as many moral catastrophes as groups that don't.

One youth leader couple shared that their marriage was in trouble. The team kept this in confidence and prayed for this couple. One of the staff members offered to pay for marital counseling, another invited the couple to go with him (at his expense) to a marriage renewal weekend. A year later, the troubled couple said, "If it weren't for the accountability and care from this team, we would be divorced today! We feel loved and cared for by you. Thanks."

Now that's a team worth being on!

Endnotes

1. Stephen R. Covey, *Principle-Centered Leadership* (New York: Simon & Schuster, Inc., 1992), 249.

2. Covey, *Principle-Centered Leadership,* 244.

3. Covey, *Principle-Centered Leadership,* 246.

4. Max Depree, *Leadership Is an Art* (New York: Bantam Doubleday Dell Publishing Group, Inc., 1989), 25.

5. Alan Loy McGinnis, *Bringing Out the Best in People* (Minneapolis, MN: Augsburg Publishing House, 1985), 136-137.

6. Denis Waitley, *The Double Win* (Old Tappan, NJ: Fleming H. Revell Company, 1985), 202.

7. Tim Smith, *Guy Stuff or It's OK to Ask for Directions* (Chicago, IL: Moody Press, 1998), 91.

8. Robert Waterman, *The Renewal Factor* (New York: Bantam Doubleday Dell Publishing Group, Inc, 1987), 336.

9. Jerry White, *Dangers Men Face* (Colorado Springs, CO: NavPress, 1997), 94.

10. Jim Marian, *Growing Up Christian* (Wheaton, IL: Victor Books, 1992), 112-114.

G R O U P   D I S C U S S I O N   Q U E S T I O N S
Chapter 8: *Collective Soul*
Nurture Your Soul Through Community

1. Have you ever had the experience of making progress but going in the wrong direction? Compare stories.

2. How does being effective differ from being efficient?

3. How does leadership differ from management?

4. How do we reconcile individuality with a sense of team?

5. How do the following five paradigm shifts help promote team spirit and synergy?
   - from program to people
   - from production to principles
   - from past to future
   - from obstacles to opportunities
   - from fear of criticism to cultural relevance

6. What are some ways we can nurture our souls individually that will help build community?

7. Study "The Effective Team Leader" list on page 118. Pick three qualities you currently are using and three you'd like to develop this year. Discuss with your group ways you can grow in these three areas while maintaining your the qualities you have.

In Search of Sabbath

Nurture Your Soul With a
Commitment to Personal Renewal

The house was silent as I pulled my dinner from the microwave oven. It was ten o'clock on Sunday evening by the time I sat down with my nuked potato, and I was famished. It had been a full day of teaching, interacting, leading meetings, and speaking at our high school meeting. I felt as if all I had been doing was talking and giving all day. I was totally drained, on empty, and irritable. I was glad that Suzanne, my wife, had gone to bed—that probably saved an argument.

As I stared out the front window, I realized I was in trouble. I couldn't keep up this pace and expect my life, marriage, and ministry to hold together. As a father,

I was beginning to understand the need to model balance to my daughters and be available to them. Taking a deeper look into my soul, I wasn't pleased. Underneath the facade of church chat and holy hype was a heart that was cynical, aloof, and cold toward God. It hadn't happened overnight—I had drifted away from a personal relationship with God in somewhat the same way partners in a marriage can become alienated through a passive neglect of the relationship. God was a stranger to me, although I referred to him often. Of course, it was on a professional basis that I referred to God, not a personal basis. The danger of full-time youth work is that it can become a job, not a journey. The spiritual discovery gets traded in for participation in a religious recreation regimen.

As I scraped the last piece of cheddar cheese from the paper plate, I searched the recesses of my empty spirit. How I longed for the days when my heart was passionate for the things of God. *How had I lost it? Couldn't I see what was happening?* It was on that brisk winter night that I told God, and myself, that I was going to do something about the cold barrenness of my soul.

My pursuit to rekindle my passion for God led me to discover a key principle: Effective ministry starts from the inside out. Ministry is more passion than profession. It's as much who we are as what we do. In all that goes on in youth ministry, spiritual energy is always required. I had been living and working as if this premise were not true. I was counting on my determination and my energy level to get me through. I hadn't recharged my own soul, and I was trying to minister out of my emptiness.

In his discussion of spiritual passion, Gordon MacDonald wrote that the supply of energy, or passion, within the inner spirit is not inexhaustible. It can and will be depleted. Young men and women tend not to know that. They surmise that the brute strength of their physical energy level can carry them on indefinitely. It can work for a while. But not forever! One day, having ignored this possibility, they awake to the extreme inner stress of exhaustion of spirit. It's a terribly confusing experience. [1]

I was perplexed because I assumed that, if I served God by doing all this youth work, he would recharge me spiritually and keep me plugged into his providential power pack. I felt disappointed with God because I was working so hard for him and he didn't seem to appreciate it. And I felt irritated with God because he had given me the ministry responsibility but not the perseverance and strength to pull it off.

As I took a harder look, I saw the confusion, the disappointment, the anger, and the blaming—and I realized I was drained. I had seen this before in myself, usually after a successful camp or some great spiritual victory in the youth group. The depression desert followed the mountaintop celebration.

I'm learning that it's not God's responsibility to keep me charged up spiritually—it's mine. For years I thought God wanted my work. It turns out he wants me! He can get his work done with or without me, but God desires intimacy with me. Ministry is designed to drive us *to* God, not away from him. Ministry is challenging and draining because God wants us to depend on him for our renewal and strength.

It's so easy to let the demands of youth work crowd in and leave no time for spiritual renewal. We want to do well, we want to be considered successful, so we run harder and longer to get the job done. But the desire for achievement is a subtle distraction from the real thing.

As Paul Borthwick noted, "When worldly success dominates our thinking, we focus our attention on power. We try to orchestrate situations that put us in the best light, rather than simply serving and leaving our reputation in God's hands. The temptation to be successful was the third temptation of Jesus. After showing Jesus all the kingdoms of the world and their splendor, the Devil said, 'All this I will give you if you will bow down and worship me' (Matthew 4:9). 'Circumvent God's way, sacrifice your priorities, and I will give you success beyond belief,' says the Devil—to Jesus and to us."[2]

There are no shortcuts to spiritual vitality. Spiritual life is an organic relationship that takes time. You have to grow it; it can't be rushed. Be suspicious of any voice promising shortcuts to spiritual success. It may be the voice of the deceiver. Spiritual growth needs to be viewed with a long-term perspective. Personal renewal is not some quick fix; it's a lifelong process. It isn't manipulation of the variables; it's a walk behind the Good Shepherd.

True spirituality isn't simply how we behave; in fact, it has more to do with *being* than behavior. Renewal of the soul can't be quantified; it's a qualitative experience that is difficult to describe, let alone measure. Teilhard de Chardin said, "We are not human beings having a spiritual experience. We are spiritual beings having a human experience." The challenge is getting back to the spiritual priority.

Private Defeats Follow Public Victories

I have discovered that private defeats follow public victories. I am most depressed or drained following a momentous occasion in the youth group. I find myself feeling alone and defeated. I'm not sure how much is emotional and how much is spiritual—I'm sure much of it is physical fatigue—but I feel down.

I used to take Monday off and stumble through the day trying to recover from my Sunday ordeal. Then I realized I was giving myself and my family my worst day. I decided to switch my day off to Friday (Thursday if we have youth activities), and instantly I discovered energy for my day off that I hadn't had in years. I now give Monday to recovering quietly by reading and doing easy tasks around the office, such as catching up with my correspondence. I find that on Monday I care about people but don't want to be with them, so I write notes to students, staff, parents, and friends. After a day of being in "recharge mode" and not taking many calls or appointments, I'm ready to face the week. Monday is a great day to be in the office if you're a youth pastor—you don't get many calls because everyone thinks you have the day off! If you're a volunteer youth worker, it's important that you, too, carve out time in your busy schedule to recharge after intense times of ministry.

Just as I have discovered that private defeats follow public victories, I have also found that private victories precede public victories. If we expect to see spiritual victories in our youth group, we will need to experience them personally first.

Someone once told me, "You can't take youth beyond where you are spiritually." As I thought about this, I realized I need to be experiencing my own spiritual growth and renewal before I can expect either from my youth group. I needed to have personal, private victories before I could experience public victories.

Stephen Covey, in *Principle-Centered Leadership,* presents the idea that principle-centered leaders exercise for self-renewal; it's a discipline of their daily lives. This isn't simply physical exercise, but mental, emotional, and spiritual, as well.

"I'm convinced that if a person will spend one hour a day on these basic exercises, he or she will improve the quality, productivity, and satisfaction of every other hour of the day, including the depth and restfulness of sleep.

"No other single hour of your day will return as much as the hour you invest in sharpening the saw, that is, in exercising these four dimensions of the human personality…We must never get too busy sawing to take time to sharpen the saw, never too busy driving to take time to get gas…If I do this hour of exercise early in the morning, it is like a private victory and just about guarantees public victories throughout the day. But if I take the course of least resistance and neglect all or part of this program, I forfeit that private victory and find myself uprooted by public pressures and stresses through the day."[3]

Stephen Covey is advocating a self-discipline that was modeled by Jesus. "Very early in the morning, while it was still dark, Jesus got up, left the house and went off to a solitary place, where he prayed" (Mark 1:35).

Jesus faced pressure-packed days. To prepare for them, he started early by spending time with his Father. In the midst of the breathless pace of bringing to life a dead girl, feeding the five thousand, and dodging the sword of King Herod, we find Jesus quietly breathing prayers to his Father. As he looked to the heavens, he received the focus and the solitude he needed for the day. Jesus was fully God and fully man, but he still needed a place for renewal. Even the Son of God needed a quiet place to recharge. Christ not only models this discipline, he encourages his faithful followers to do the same.

"The apostles gathered around Jesus and reported to him all they had done and taught. Then, because so many people were coming and going that they did not even have a chance to eat, he said to them, 'Come with me by yourselves to a quiet place and get some rest.' So they went away by themselves in a boat to a solitary place" (Mark 6:30-32).

The apostles were excited about the miracles and the "growth in the program." They focused on what "they had done and taught." Jesus knew the danger of being excited and busy and focusing on our own accomplishments. He knew it was a recipe for burnout. The apostles had been so swamped with meeting needs and being surrounded by people that they hadn't taken the time to rest and renew. I think it's interesting to see that Jesus didn't say, "That's great, guys! Wow! We fed four thousand! Let's try for five thousand today!" Christ could have pushed for performance, but he called them to rest.

That's my concern for you, dear youth worker. Do you find yourself wrapped up in "what you have done and taught"? Is your excitement in your performance or in the Person? Jesus would call you, faithful follower, and say, "Come with me by yourself. Leave your calendar, your book of crowdbreakers, and your camp planning. Let's go to a quiet place where we can rest." Do you hear him?

As I reflect on Christ's solitary times, I discover that these weren't times of preparation for the distant future, but for that day. As youth workers we often fall into the pattern of "spending time with God now because he'll use it in the future." It's really easy to imagine our dreams as God's will for our life. We think God is leading us through something because it will help us in the future. But what we see as the process, God sees as the end itself. God's purpose always involves the day at hand; he wants us to depend on him and his power for today.

Jesus pushed his disciples to get in the boat and go on ahead of him while he went up the mountain to pray (Mark 6:45). As the storm whipped the lake into a white-capped froth, Jesus came strolling by, walking on the water. He had almost passed them when they spotted him and cried out. In the middle of the storms of life, Jesus wants us to call out to him. He wanted to teach his disciples to see him in spite of their fear and the pounding waves. That's his goal for each of us—that we should see that he can walk on the storms of our lives right now.

I found this thought expressed in Oswald Chambers' words: "God's training is for now, not later. His purpose is for this very minute, not for sometime in the future. We have nothing to do with what will follow our obedience, and we are wrong to concern ourselves with it. What people call preparation, God sees as the goal itself." [4]

It's easy to use our quiet times as preparation for the next youth group lesson. We may try to discipline ourselves from that and focus on our own renewal, only to be interrupted by the thought, "This would be a great teaching for my next series!"

To help myself combat this temptation, I have two study periods each week. Tuesday mornings are primarily what I call *personal study*. I focus on growing as a person and recharging my spirit and mind. Others have called this *offensive study*—a time to move out against the enemy by preparing as a warrior. In contrast, *defensive study* is preparing to deliver tonight's Bible study. I prefer to use the terms *personal study* and *teaching study*. My quiet times are in the morning, before my feet hit the carpet. I read Scripture, think about it, and then pray. These morning times are much more meaningful now that I have my study times. My quiet times are just for me. I don't have to prepare a lesson; I prepare my life.

I have benefited from the writings of Henri Nouwen. They have helped me nurture my soul. I now value solitude. "Without solitude it is virtually impossible to live a spiritual life. Solitude begins with a time and place for God, and Him alone." [5]

Teaching Study

My Thursday mornings are spent preparing for the teaching for the weekend. My administrative assistant holds calls for me during both of my study periods, and I don't schedule any appointments. I usually can get in all my teaching study because I'm refreshed from my personal study.

If you're a volunteer youth worker, you'll need to adjust this idea to fit your schedule. For example, you could have your personal quiet times in the morning, pick one weeknight to study for your teaching, and skip one hour of TV each week to read a good Christian book (like this one!).

If you find you're running out of teaching preparation time, it could be that you need to spend less time preparing. That's right, spend some of your teaching prep time on refreshing your own spirit. Chances are, with a renewed mind and spirit, you'll be able to comprehend and process spiritual truth much faster. I find that if I cheat on my personal study and let other things crowd in it takes me twice as long to prepare my lessons.

It's like that car repair commercial, "You can pay me now, or you can pay me later." Invest in recharging your soul now; it's a lot less expensive than recovering from total burnout.

Spiritual renewal is only part of the battle for personal renewal. Sometimes we just need a break from the pressures and demands of youth work. For those of you in full-time youth work, it's important for you to have one complete day off each week. That means not calling the office, not stopping by the church, not taking calls that deal with your work, and not socializing with church people who seem like work!

Ridge Burns offers four helpful rules for preserving your day off.

"Rule 1: I leave my work at the office on my day off." I don't take phone calls unless they're emergencies…I totally drop out of ministry to the church and minister only to my family.

"Rule 2: I plan my day off with my family one week in advance."

"Rule 3: I try not to skip my devotions on my day off." Devotions help me think more about my family. I pray for them before they get up, and that allows me to approach my day off in a more spiritual way.

"Rule 4: I am as creative on my day off as I am in youth ministry." When I think about how carefully I plan a retreat to make sure kids are entertained, ministered to, and challenged in their faith, I'm embarrassed at how little time and creative energy I spend helping my family enjoy those same kinds of experiences.[6]

Cultivating the Garden

Prior to teaching, my wife, Suzanne, completed special courses to become a state-certified master gardener. As a "colorscape" gardener, her job dealt exclusively with flowers. She is a flower expert.

One of her clients had a beautiful estate home with expensive landscaping and a huge lawn. As she began working the soil in the flower garden, she realized no one had ever amended the soil or cultivated the garden. It was ironic that this mansion of a house would have hardpan dirt in front of it. It had the potential to be in House & Garden magazine, but it wasn't living up to it.

The same is true of people. God has given us the potential to be beautiful gardens—masterpieces of his grace and care—but many of us are hardpan. We resist the trauma of being cultivated. If we want to experience God's renewing beauty, we must be willing to till our souls.

Tilling means turning over what was and exposing something new. It's an invasive interruption of the status quo. Cultivation usually involves some disruption, some form of upheaval. For many of us, the disturbance comes as suffering. We're quick to blame suffering for our lack of a nurtured soul.

"I believe our understanding is shallow. The path that truly heals and redeems begins at the point when we realize we want more perspective, purpose, and passion in life. It passes through the dark terrain of the shadow of death, through the dry desert where little makes sense and where we lose most, if not all, that seems important to us. And then it takes us to a green, verdant valley that once was Baca, the place of tears, and is now a meadow of lush joy and inconceivable pleasure. My premise is that doubt, despair, and disappointment are not only a reality of daily life, they are also tools God uses to grow faith, hope, and love in us. If we run from what we fear or find displeasurable, we actually rob ourselves of the joy God intends for us to experience as we walk through our past, play with our future, and live now with new passion."[7]

Gardening involves the following steps:
cultivating
planting
watering

waiting

protecting

harvesting

Gardening our souls for harvest requires the same process. We must be willing to let God *cultivate* our lives. That means we must let him break through the surface and till us. A tiller turns the soil over to mix the soil and add oxygen.

The same is true of our lives. God seeks to turn over that which has been unmoved. We may like it left untouched, but, for the harvest, it needs to be cultivated. We get so comfortable with the status quo that we forget that a little change is good for all growing things. To reject the discomfort of cultivation is to reject the promise of the harvest. Cultivation involves studying your present life and deciding what needs to change. It means allowing the Holy Spirit to make the necessary changes.

Planting is the second step toward a growing spirit. We need to plant seeds that will increase the potential of the harvest. Planting may involve scheduling time for exercising the disciplines for personal renewal. I try to set goals for these disciplines. Mine are exercise three times a week, get seven hours of sleep each night, make quiet times five days a week, spend four evenings per week at home, read for five hours per week (instead of watching TV), and write for five hours per week. I don't always achieve these goals, but I'm increasing my harvest potential by planting seeds of renewal.

Watering represents the daily adding of input for renewal in my life. This may mean choosing to listen to positive, uplifting music instead of the news. It may mean eating lunch by myself in the park and enjoying the beauty of God's creation. I water my soul by meditating on God's Word and reflecting on his past faithfulness. Through prayer and positive reminders, I water my soul daily.

Waiting is often overlooked, but it's an integral part of growth. Waiting gives us time to give up our agenda to discover God's. It allows us the time to develop relationships with others who will support us and share with us. When we're waiting, we have time for dialogue. As we discuss our thoughts, we process information and begin to expand ourselves. A relaxed, authentic conversation gives each person a feeling of being more alive, with more capacity, than before the dialogue. This kind of growth can't be rushed. We need to learn the value of patience if we're to maximize the lessons that can be learned only in God's waiting room.

Protecting refers to keeping ourselves safe. Certain environments and people could be destructive to us. If we want a harvest, we have to take some precautions. We need to evaluate everything coming into our garden, screening for bugs and rodents and protecting the garden against disease. Some fungi can be deadly to a hybrid rose. We just can't say "yes" to everything that wants to come into our garden (life). We need some boundaries, and we have to say "no" to many good things so we can say "yes" to the best. The best protection for our soul gardens is prayer. It is our sentry against the garden's enemies.

I appreciate the honesty of John Ortberg on the topic of prayer. "What I have come to realize, over time, is that brief times of focused prayer interspersed with these wanderings is all my mind is capable of at this point. One day I hope to do better. But for now, I find consolation in the words of Brother Lawrence: 'For many years I was bothered by the thought that I was a failure at prayer. Then one day I realized I would always be a failure at prayer; and I've gotten along much better ever since.'" [8]

Harvesting is the reward for those who are willing to work the gardens of their souls. It's the time, energy, creativity, and fruit of our labor. It's a prized blossom we cherish and bring glory to. In youth work, the harvest is the change in our youth. It's the observable growth, the increased joy, the application of God's truth, and the experience of renewal or life-change. Different crops will mature at different times; people will find that the harvest comes in different seasons. If we follow the law of the harvest, we'll nurture growth and renewal in our own souls first, then in the gardens of our young people.

"Being confident of this, that he who began a good work in you will carry it on to completion until the day of Christ Jesus. It is right for me to feel this way about all of you, since I have you in my heart…and this is my prayer: that your love may abound more and more in knowledge and depth and insight, so that you may be able to discern what is best and may be pure and blameless until the day of Christ, filled with the fruit of righteousness that comes through Jesus Christ—to the glory and praise of God" (Philippians 1:6-7a, 9-11).

I am confident that God will continue to nurture your soul. It will be by his power and in his time. Then you'll experience his harvest—the "fruit of righteousness."

Success is reaching goals that benefit ourselves and others. We'll be effective in our youth work when we, with nurtured souls, leave a legacy of contribution and growth.

How do you measure success?
To laugh often and much;
To win the respect of intelligent people
and the affection of children;
To earn the appreciation of honest critics
and endure the betrayal of false friends;
To appreciate beauty;
To find the best in others;
To leave the world a bit better,
whether by a healthy child, a garden patch,
a redeemed social condition, or a job well done;
To know even one other life has breathed easier
because you have lived—
This is to have succeeded.

—*Ralph Waldo Emerson*

Endnotes

1. Gordon MacDonald, *Restoring Your Spiritual Passion* (Nashville, TN: Thomas Nelson Publishers Inc.,1986), 40.

2. Paul Borthwick, *Feeding Your Forgotten Soul* (Grand Rapids, MI: Zondervan Publishing House, 1990), 36.

3. Stephen R. Covey, *Principle-Centered Leadership* (New York: Simon & Schuster, Inc., 1992), 38-39.

4. Oswald Chambers, *My Utmost for His Highest* (Grand Rapids, MI: Discovery House Publishers, 1992), July 28 devotion.

5. Henri J. M. Nouwen, *Out of Solitude: Three Meditations on the Christian Life* (Notre Dame, IN: Ave Maria Press, 1984), 14.

6. Ridge Burns, *No Youth Worker Is an Island* (Wheaton, IL: Victor Books, 1992), 156.

7. Dan B. Allender, Ph.D., *The Healing Path* (Colorado Springs, CO: WaterBrook Press, 1999), Preface.

8. John Ortberg, *The Life You've Always Wanted* (Grand Rapids, MI: Zondervan Publishing House, 1997), 96.

GROUP DISCUSSION QUESTIONS
Chapter 9: *In Search of Sabbath*

Nurture Your Soul With a Commitment to Personal Renewal

1. How do you feel when you're burned out? How do you react and relate to others?

2. How have you experienced the maxim, "Effective ministry starts from the inside out"?

3. Describe a time when a private defeat followed a public victory.

4. What kind of environment and experience are renewing for you? Why?

5. Review the six steps for gardening the soul. Explore and expand on the definitions. Which of these do you think would help you nurture your soul?

    cultivating, planting, watering, waiting, protecting, harvesting

6. What practical actions might develop the quality of renewal in your life?

Soul Work

Beginning the Process of Nurture

Youth ministry is more about passion than profession. You may not have all the technical skills or the seminary degree, but, if you love your students, they'll know it.

If you have the gift of preaching expositionally accurate sermons in Greek, the ability to fathom all the mysteries of Hebrew, thorough knowledge of software and the Web, and a youth budget the size of a mountain, but have not love, you are nothing!

It's through love that you'll connect teenagers with God, and it's your love that God wants. Consider the words of Brother Lawrence, a monk who learned to enjoy God's presence as he scrubbed pots and pans. "We ought not to be weary of doing little things for the love of God, who regards not the greatness of the work, but the love with which it is performed." [1]

The value of our youth ministry can't be judged by its size. God wouldn't say, "I am amazed at all the kids in your youth group! I'm really impressed with your program." He couldn't care less about our programs. He cares about our souls.

But keeping love in the performance of what we do means nurturing the soul. A nurtured soul is a loving soul. A loving soul is what we need for effective youth ministry.

Effective leaders come from a variety of backgrounds and personalities, but they tend to have common qualities that make them effective. In the preceding chapters, we've explored eight ways to nurture your soul. We've learned that effectiveness is an internal issue more than an external one. Who we *are* has much influence on how effective we are. *Being* impacts *doing*.

Youth workers who are effective don't simply know the "secrets" of youth ministry, they've developed personal habits that translate into powerful patterns. They're women and men of vision who can transform their vision into reality.

Nurturing your soul will take regular application of the principles suggested in the previous chapters. It will require healthy patterns of behavior, habits that nurture. Habits are sometimes easy to fall into, difficult to develop, and near impossible to break. They can be good or bad. In this book, we focused on developing positive habits that nurture our souls. But, to be more effective with your new habits, you may need to be liberated from some old habits. Old patterns, perspectives, and paradigms may be keeping you from nurturing fresh and vital habits. "Forget the former things; do not dwell on the past. See, I am doing a new thing! Now it springs up; do you not perceive it?" (Isaiah 43:18-19)

Dr. Denis Waitley says that habits are fragile at first and can easily be broken—like cobwebs. But in time, and with practice, they can be like cables—giving support and strength to your life. That's our goal—from cobwebs to cables! [2]

If we're going to change youth for eternity, we'll need internalized habits that will empower us toward effectiveness. We'll need souls that are healthy and nurtured. Effective youth work is an internal issue.

We live in a culture that is rapidly becoming discouraged with hype and the personality ethic. We're in search of quality—from the inside out. As youth workers, we're in a privileged position because we can help shape the next generation into one that is committed to growth in character. The best place to start is with ourselves.

I was speaking to seven hundred high school winter campers, and I asked them to complete my sentence, "If it's worth doing, it's…" To my amazement, all seven hundred echoed in unison, "worth doing well." I teased them about having the same mother and father and asked them why they all would parrot the same line. "Have you been brainwashed?" I quizzed.

Where do we get this idea that if it's "worth doing, it's worth doing well?" If something is *worth* doing, it's worth doing poorly or with mediocrity!

I asked the campers to chant after me, "If it's worth doing, it's worth doing with mediocrity." They laughed and filed it in their memories to use with their parents, but there was an immense liberty that came over that camp. Many of those students were living in families and coming from youth groups that were performance-based and perfectionistic.

If something is worth doing, *just do it!* Don't worry about the results.

One of my favorite movies is *What About Bob?* Bob, played by Bill Murray, discovers liberation from some of his perfectionistic obsessions and begins a process of growth. He learns "baby steps"—small steps in the right direction to help him through one day at a time.

I want you to baby step with these principles for soul nurture. They're worth doing with mediocrity. In time, you'll develop them into stronger patterns and you'll do them with more regularity. Then they'll become so personalized that you'll have a difficult time separating yourself from the habits. We become our habits.

Don't try to develop all eight nurturing habits at once. Choose one to work on at a time. Use the discussion questions to stimulate learning with other youth workers.

Changing cobwebs into cables takes time and personal discipline. But it's better to choose the cables that build strength into your life than to be bound to the cables that imprison you.

The Perseverance of Nurture

Nurturing takes time. We live in a hurry-up world. I get annoyed when down-loading a document from the Internet takes longer than two minutes. A few years ago, in the age of faxes, sending a document used to take five minutes (including the time to send and check to see if it was received). A few years before that, we had to wait a day to get an urgent message (and pay dearly for it!). Technology is making us impatient.

A new day planner and some courses on time management aren't enough. Simply reorganizing our lives with quick-fix, external adjustment isn't enough. Henri Nouwen captured how most of us feel when he wrote, "One of the most obvious characteristics of our daily lives is that we are busy. We experience our days as filled with things to do, people to meet, projects to finish, letters to write, calls to make, and appointments to keep. Our lives often seem like over-packed suitcases bursting at the seams. In fact, we are almost always aware of being behind schedule. There is a nagging sense that there are unfinished tasks, unfulfilled promises, unrealized proposals. There is always something else that we should have remembered, done, or said. There are always people we did not speak to, write to, or visit. Thus, although we are very busy, we also have a lingering feeling of never really fulfilling our obligations."[3]

If you're lacking motivation to nurture your soul, consider the window of time you have to reach students. The window is shrinking. We have less and less time to influence youth. We must be more effective. Our teenagers have less time for youth ministry—even they seem to be rushed.

I wanted to schedule a time to meet with one of our high school students.

"Let me see when I can work you in," he said, pulling out a state-of-the-art, palm-size electronic organizer. "How does a week from Tuesday sound?"

I fumbled with my trusty leather and paper Day-Timer, "Sure, that will be fine." *He was busier than I was!*

Most of us are living life with little or no margin. You've probably heard about the doctor who called his patient and said, "I have bad news. You have twenty-four hours to live."

"Oh, that's terrible!" the patient cried.

"But I have even worse news," cautioned the doctor.

"What could be worse than having only twenty-four hours to live?"

"I have been trying to call you since yesterday!"

Our dog acted like a rabbit. Not just any old rabbit, but the White Rabbit from Walt Disney's version of *Alice in Wonderland*. Remember that manic bunny? Spinning his legs in rapid rotations per minute, but not really getting anywhere. Bingo acted like the White Rabbit. We went for a drive and put Bingo, our Labrador retriever, in the back of our Trooper. He loved to ride in the back and stick his head out the window. For years, he would ride with us and let the wind blow his black ears back and draw up his flaring nostrils. He looked like he thought he was flying.

This Saturday, on the way to a sporting event, he leaned too far and fell out. I was driving at least thirty-five miles per hour.

I heard our daughter scream, "Bingo fell out! Stop, daddy!"

I turned around and didn't see Bingo, but I did see the end of his leash still hooked to the inside of the Trooper. I checked my right side mirror. I could see Bingo running very fast next to the car, inches from the tire. Every few feet, he would hop off the pavement and fly for a few feet, then he would land and keep running. The treadmill never stopped. Even in the air, his paws speedily cranked RPMs. He still wore his collar and leash. It had kept him strapped close to the car. It was a matter of survival. He knew he had to run fast or risk getting run over or dragged at thirty-five miles per hour.

I slammed on the brakes and skidded to a stop. But Bingo doesn't have brakes. He flew past us until his leash ran out! It snagged him with a jerk and grounded him.

"I have killed our dog." I was in a panic as I ran to check on him.

Surprisingly, he was OK—scared, but OK, except for minor cuts and scrapes and heat blisters on the pads of his paws from running for his life. He wasn't interested in car rides for a long time.

Sometimes we're like Bingo, desperately running to keep up. We often run without a purpose. We may be running with intensity but without direction.

May I suggest taking a break? That's what God had in mind when he commanded us to honor the Sabbath (Exodus 20:8). He knew that we need a rest from our labor. We need time to reflect, refresh, and redirect ourselves. We need time set apart (sanctified) for worship. The Sabbath isn't about time off, it's about sacred time.

Dr. Laura Schlessinger speaks to millions on the radio. In a recent book, she reminds us of the value of Sabbath. "As you conquer and create all week long, it's all too easy to get an inflated and self-centered idea of your own power. Egocentrism often takes us away from doing and being for others and God in a way that brings our life meaning and serves a greater purpose than our personal gratification and acquisition. Having to stop is not just about recovering from exhaustion from a hard week's work. Sabbath is about standing back and viewing our life, in the way an artist stands back from his canvas to get a more encompassing view of his work. This gives us the opportunity to contemplate the merits of our contribution to others and the world—it is about resetting our spiritual clock. The kind of Sabbath 'rest' that is of value is that which reconnects you to your ultimate purpose in life."[4]

I know it's difficult for youth workers to take Sunday off. Sunday may be the longest day of our work week. We need to develop an alternative Sabbath; perhaps it's Saturday or Monday. But determine one day a week you'll set aside for Sabbath. Consider these Sabbath activities:

- listening to praise music
- reading an inspirational book
- going on a walk and observing God's handiwork
- writing a letter of praise to God
- worshiping at a service or with friends
- reading the Bible
- reflecting on God's goodness
- taking a break from projects around the house
- praying
- meditating
- writing in a journal
- doing nothing—being still, listening
- conversing with family members
- being by yourself; learning the discipline of solitude
- enjoying fellowship

I like Dr. Laura's advice about standing back and looking at the canvas of our lives. We need to take time to discover what the Master has done in our lives. It takes time and quiet to notice his hand in our lives.

Consider God's promise to Zephaniah: "The Lord your God is with you, he is mighty to save. He will take great delight in you, he will quiet you with his love, he will rejoice over you with singing" (Zephaniah 3:17).

An evidence of God's might is quiet. It's just the opposite in our world. We have confused the mighty with the noisy, the important with the complex, and direction with frantic activity.

If we're to nurture our souls, it will require time to be quieted by God's love. It's in the stillness that we hear the music in our souls.

"Shhh…can you hear it?…Wait…It's our Father rejoicing over us. He is singing *our song*.

The Direction of Nurture

A nurtured soul requires spiritual direction. In a culture bent on chaos, it's mandatory that we take time to order our souls. We need to take time to direct our private world.

Dan Allender—counselor, professor, and author—writes, "A radical life is committed to disturbing and drawing others to God. Further, a radical life is willing to be directed and also to direct others on the healing path, where they will grow in faith, hope and love.

"One of the most thrilling movements in the church is a return to spiritual direction, silence, and simplicity. One friend said of her church, 'There is so little silence between the words that I drown in all the noise. I leave and need to go sit for hours to rest from all the frenetic activity of worship.'

"Noise. A radio in my daughter's room, my son is watching TV, and I write as I listen to Van Morrison. I'm more afraid of silence than I am of cacophony. Silence brings us face to face with our greatest fears and our deepest desires—most of us prefer noise and distractions to quiet centeredness." [5]

Sometimes the noise is an escape. The activity is simply a diversion. If we are to nurture our souls, we'll need to be quiet and still. In the stillness we hear our Father's direction.

"Come be with me…Let that go. Embrace me…Cease from your labor. Enjoy me…Be still, and know that I am God."

We need to be still for ourselves. We need to model stillness for our students.

Students are busy. They have less time and higher expectations. Many of them reflect the culture with a "What have you done for me lately?" attitude. They are drop-in-service oriented. They expect quality and service in the limited time they have. They truly are products of the consumer generation.

What is our response to this?

Some youth workers lament the days gone by—the "golden days of youth work when we had time with the youth." Others become angry or bitter and accuse teenagers of being selfish and materialistic.

A healthier response might be to become more effective with the time we *do* have. We need to minister from the inside out with souls that are full, healthy, and renewed. A nurtured soul will have a greater impact on youth than a snappy program.

Youth workers committed to personal growth are dependent on the Holy Spirit. They know the qualities they seek to develop come out of a vital, dependent relationship with God. They don't seek to manufacture the fruit; the fruit comes as a result of abiding in the Vine. This perspective allows youth workers to view adversity with new confidence. Instead of running from difficult times or seeing them as sources of doubt, they can see them as sources for growth. The wise youth worker understands that God uses adversity to develop character that couldn't be developed in times of comfort and ease.

"There is an ache in every soul. No matter how good life has been to us, we want what only heaven can provide. No matter how deeply we deny or attempt to escape our hunger for God, it can't help but haunt the narrative of our stories. It may not come to the surface as a clear and direct hunger for the transcendent, but our need for God is part of the genetic structure of every desire, whether legitimate and good or dark and decadent. We must develop the skill to hear and pursue desire, because desire reveals what the seeking heart most deeply pursues."[6]

Does your soul ache for God? Do you desire him as you do food? When you have time to think without being distracted, what does your mind go to? Chances are, this is your desire.

Buddy System

A word of caution: Do not attempt to nurture your soul on your own. (Kids, don't try this at home!) You need the support and encouragement of at least one other person. When Jesus sent out his disciples, he sent them out in twos. Find a "buddy" who can be your soul growth mate.

You'll need someone to bear with you. A friend, according to one definition, is "someone who walks in when everyone else walks out." You'll need a friend committed to the growth of your soul and of his or her own. "Bearing with one another" means learning to listen to God speak through one another. It means learning to listen for God through difficult people and in difficult situations. It is learning to hang in there and *be there* for people when you would rather walk out.

When I learn to stick it out, to stay when I would rather leave, I learn that the most challenging person to be devoted to is one who has the same struggles that seethe in my soul. It is in the perseverance and the listening that I discover that the most difficult person I have to deal with is *me*.

There is much going on around us that is toxic to our own personal spiritual vitality, as well as to that of our youth. The pace of life causes us to quickly become unbalanced and forget the other side of the spectrum. It's easy to ignore our spouses, our children, and our physical and spiritual health in the rush to perform as youth workers. The competing demands make us vulnerable to destruction from within and without.

A burned out youth worker becomes vulnerable to the world, the flesh, and the devil. Because we're engaged in spiritual warfare, we need to keep ourselves renewed and growing on the cutting edge.

As we step into a new millennium, young people are looking for a cause to join. They're seeking a purpose they can embrace with their heads, hearts, and hands. We can offer them a model of an explorer on a great adventure. We can present the cosmic drama of all time—the mystery of the gospel—Christ in us and the hope of glory! This drama is significant—a cause worth living for.

The new millennium lies before us like a blank white board.

Youth are searching; they're wondering, "What will be important in the year 2020?" and "What should I live my life for in this new time?"

As youth workers, we are shapers of the next generation. We are pioneers of the new millennium. We have within our grasp the tools to build a mighty team of youth who may impact our culture and the world as no other generation has.

It begins with us. It begins from within. It begins with our souls.

Endnotes

1. Brother Lawrence, *The Practice of the Presence of God* (Uhrichsville, OH: Barbour and Company, Inc., 1993), 29.

2. Denis Waitley, *The Psychology of Winning* audiocassette series (Niles, IL: Nightingale-Conant Corporation, 1993).

3. Henri J. M. Nouwen, *Making All Things New* (San Francisco: Harper, 1981), 23-24.

4. Dr. Laura Schlessinger and Rabbi Stewart Vogel, *The Ten Commandments: The Significance of God's Laws in Everyday Life* (New York: HarperCollins Publishers, Inc., 1998), 104-105.

5. Allender, Ph.D., *The Healing Path* (Colorado Springs, CO: WaterBrook Press, 1999), 203.

6. Allender, Ph.D., *The Healing Path,* 224.

GROUP DISCUSSION QUESTIONS
Chapter 10: *Soul Work*

Beginning the Process of Nurture

1. Which of the chapters/principles are relevant to your youth ministry today? Explain.

2. Why do you think some youth workers *know* what to do, but have a difficult time *implementing* what they know?

3. In what ways can old habits and perspectives keep you from nurturing your soul?

4. In what ways do we as youth workers "dwell on the past" and miss the new thing God wants to do (Isaiah 43:18-19)?

5. What do you think about the advice, "If it's worth doing, it's worth doing with mediocrity"?

6. What are some "baby steps" you could take to begin applying *one* of these nurturing habits to your life?

7. Who will help you with support and encouragement as you learn to walk with your renewed zeal for nurturing your soul?

Self-Evaluation Exercises

Self-Evaluation Exercises

CHAPTER 2

Nurture Your Soul With a Commitment to Lifelong Learning

Take the following test to see how committed you are to lifelong learning. Mark one response for each statement.

	Usually	Sometimes	Usually Not
1. I am aware of the trends that affect youth culture.	❑	❑	❑
2. I see life's experiences as opportunities for learning.	❑	❑	❑
3. During a conversation, I listen as much as I talk.	❑	❑	❑
4. If ministry is finding a need and meeting it, I have a strategy to adjust my ministry as needs in the culture change.	❑	❑	❑
5. I can point to failures that have been my teachers.	❑	❑	❑
6. I have others around me to give me input and keep me balanced.	❑	❑	❑
7. I see the changes in our culture as opportunities to reach people's spiritual needs.	❑	❑	❑

Scoring: Give yourself a **1** for each "Usually Not," a **2** for each "Sometimes," and a **3** for each "Usually."

7-11	You've been ditching class.
12-15	Welcome to the elementary school of life.
16-17	Congratulations on graduating into the University of Life.
18-21	You have developed learning as a life skill. Way to go!

CHAPTER 3
Nurture Your Soul by Serving

Use the following questions to evaluate how service-oriented you are.

1. How would you rate your youth work?

Consistent	❏
Distinctive	❏
User-friendly	❏
Responsive	❏
Offering Value	❏

2. Which of the following four ways to empower through serving are strong or weak in your youth ministry?

	Strong	Weak
A. Students discover significance in serving.	❏	❏
B. Students are empowered by competence.	❏	❏
C. Students feel they are a part of a community.	❏	❏
D. Fun is part of our service projects.	❏	❏

3. Which of the following assumptions have you had? How have they influenced your view of service and outreach?

A. Teenagers need to be entertained.

B. Teenagers don't want to be challenged.

C. Our teenagers don't have non-Christian friends.

D. Everyone in our group is a Christian.

E. Teenagers would rather play than serve.

4. To help you draw "outside the lines," respond to the following:

What have we done in the past that was successful?

Are we a slave to the things we've done in the past?

Has it become a dinosaur?

What might a new approach look like—one that is totally different in style but will achieve the same purpose?

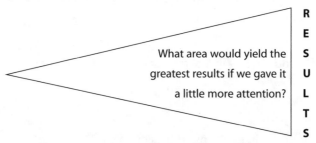

What area would yield the **R E S U L T S** greatest results if we gave it a little more attention?

What seems impossible but, if it could be done, would have an incredible impact?

5. Use this Ten Ways to Serve list to evaluate yourself. Draw a face for each response.

Always   Sometimes   Seldom

1. Return all phone calls within twenty-four hours.
2. Call or e-mail students for no reason, just to say hi.
3. Give parents complete information about the details of events.
4. Take at least one student to lunch each month.
5. Do more listening than talking.
6. Go to student recitals or events that few people attend.
7. Spend time with youth volunteers.
8. Survey your students' needs.
9. Become a partner with the parents of your students.
10. Set a goal to serve a student at each level.

C H A P T E R   4
Nurture Your Soul by Radiating the Positive Power of the Holy Spirit

1. What do you think it means to "overflow with hope by the power of the Holy Spirit" (Romans 15:13)?

2. What might you observe in a person under the influence of the Holy Spirit?

3. Which of these qualities is most appealing to you?

4. How would this appealing quality assist you in youth ministry?

5. Study the chart contrasting the Personality ethic with the Character ethic on page 54. Which quality under the character ethic would you most like to see evident in your life?

6. What could you do to develop this character quality, or the desired quality of the Holy Spirit in your life?

7. Describe the steps you can take beginning this week.

CHAPTER 5
Nurture Your Soul by Believing in Others and Their Growth

Evaluate your ministry team using the ten tips for empowering your team with vision.

	1 Never	2 Seldom	3 Sometimes	4 Often	5 Always
1. Develop a vision statement that captures your vision.	❏	❏	❏	❏	❏
2. Regularly communicate your vision statement to your team.	❏	❏	❏	❏	❏
3. Expect the best from your team members.	❏	❏	❏	❏	❏
4. Know the needs of your students and team members.	❏	❏	❏	❏	❏
5. Establish high standards of excellence.	❏	❏	❏	❏	❏
6. Learn from failure.	❏	❏	❏	❏	❏
7. Promote team spirit (minimize competition).	❏	❏	❏	❏	❏
8. Encourage and model personal renewal.	❏	❏	❏	❏	❏
9. Celebrate achievement and growth.	❏	❏	❏	❏	❏
10. Balance ministry and life (be able to say no).	❏	❏	❏	❏	❏

Scoring: Give yourself the appropriate value for each response (**1** for Never, **2** for Seldom, and so on), and add up the marks for each column.

10-19   Do you have a team?
20-30   You have a start on building your team.
31-40   You obviously are on a growing team.
41-50   Wow! You are on a world-class empowered team!

CHAPTER 6
Nurture Your Soul With Balance

1. Are you more of a "911 Nancy" (seven-day-a-week youth worker) or a "Phil Family Man" (my family always comes first)?

   Explain how each youth worker would handle the following scenario:

   > It's 11:00 p.m. and you're ready for bed. The phone rings and it's Lance, one of the kids in the youth group: "I need to talk with you right now because my parents are being cruel to me. They're totally insane! I hate them!"
   >
   > "What's the problem?"
   >
   > "I don't want to talk about it over the phone, can I come over?"

   How would 911 Nancy respond?

   How would Phil Family Man respond?

2. Make a list of how much time you spend each week in the following competitive time demands.

   Amount of time

   Personal time

   Ministry time

   Thought time

   Activity time

   Time with adults

   Time with students

   Time with parents

3. What would the ideal balanced week look like to you?

	Amount of Time	**What Would You Do?**
Personal time		
Ministry time		
Thought time		
Activity time		
Time with adults		
Time with students		
Time with parents		

4. Make an ideal weekly schedule that reflects this ideal balance. Experiment with it for a week and then revise it.

Sunday	Monday	Tuesday	Wednesday	Thursday	Friday	Saturday

CHAPTER 7
Nurture Your Soul With Risk

1. What makes life an adventure for you?

2. There are three ways to approach life's journey: as a traveler, a tourist, or an explorer.

   A traveler just wants to get to the destination. He or she is focused on getting to a stopping place to rest.

   The tourist enjoys stopping by the side of the road at scenic spots and enjoying the view. He or she might take a picture, have a picnic, and then get back on the highway.

   The explorer loves to leave the road most traveled and explore regions unknown. He or she sees life as an adventure and is willing to climb a few mountains to capture the view from the summit.

   What might each of the people described above do in the following situation?

   Your reputation as a youth worker has reached Latin America, and you have been asked to visit one of your sister churches in Guatemala. "Would you please come to Guatemala and tell us about effective youth work? We will pay for you, your spouse, and one of your key student leaders to come and help us."

   You consider the two-week mission: "All expenses paid and a unique opportunity for me, my spouse, and one lucky kid."

   The **traveler** would…

   The **tourist** would…

   The **explorer** would…

CHAPTER 8
Nurture Your Soul Through Community

1. A producer is one who acts on new ideas and products. A manager coordinates the work and the workers. The leader sets the vision and direction for the team. Which of these roles best describes your role in youth work? Why?

2. Effective teams have discovered how to affirm each member's uniqueness. They make it their goal to make each person's strength more productive and each weakness more irrelevant. These efforts lead to synergy—the state in which the whole is more than the sum of the parts. Synergistic youth work seeks to affirm the value and contribution of each youth worker. How does this style of ministry compare to the scriptural accounts in 1 Corinthians 12 and Ephesians 4:1-16?

3. To build your team, you may need a paradigm shift. Review the material about the team builder paradigm shift on pages 110-111.

   How are you doing on the following paradigm shifts?

   From: PROGRAM to PEOPLE

   PRODUCTION to PRINCIPLES

   PAST to FUTURE

   OBSTACLES to OPPORTUNITIES

   FEAR OF CRITICISM to CULTURAL RELEVANCE

4. Take another look at the twenty qualities of the effective team leader on page 118.

   Which of these qualities are evident in your team now?

   Which of these qualities are evident some of the time, or with some of the team members?

   Which of these qualities are seldom seen on your team?

Pick two of the qualities you would like to see more of on your youth ministry team.

1.

2.

5. What could you do to help grow these two qualities of the effective team leader, in yourself and others on your team?

CHAPTER 9

Nurture Your Soul With a Commitment to Personal Renewal

Burnout Potential Quiz

Respond by recording a number that best represents the frequency of the activities listed below.

10 9 8 7 6 5 4 3 2 1

Always-Frequently-Sometimes-Seldom-Never

1. I find myself skipping meals.

2. I talk on the phone when I should be sleeping.

3. Phone calls interrupt dinner.

4. I'm out five or more nights a week.

5. I exercise less than twice a week.

6. I skip my times alone with God.

7. I overlook time for myself.

8. I have friends to support me.

9. I have a regular hobby that I enjoy.

10. I take a full day off weekly.

11. I read books for inspiration.

12. I limit the amount of TV I watch.

13. I keep a journal or take time just to think.

14. My study time is separate from my personal spiritual renewal.

Scoring

1. Add up the values from questions 1-7. Enter the total here: _____
    - 70-60 Burnout is inevitable.
    - 59-49 Burnout is likely.
    - 48-30 Fifty percent chance of burnout.
    - 29-18 You are good at personal renewal.
    - 17-7   You are totally charged. Burnout is highly unlikely.

2. Add up the values from questions 8-14. Enter the total here: _____
   70-60   You have mastered self-renewal.
   59-49   You show skill in personal renewal.
   48-30   Your personal renewal skills need strengthening
   29-18   Have you ever considered personal renewal?
   17-7   You're speeding toward destruction on the Burnout Express.

3. As a result of this information about myself, I plan to…
   (Describe a short strategy for change, if you need to.)

CHAPTER 10
Beginning the Process of Nurture

Evaluate how you are doing with the eight principles for nurturing your soul. Describe your current status under "I Am" and an idea to strengthen this area under "I Could."

	I Am	I Could

1. Nurture Requires Change
   Nurture Your Soul With a Commitment to Lifelong Learning

2. The Way Up Is Down
   Nurture Your Soul by Serving

3. Power Surge
   Nurture Your Soul by Radiating the Positive Power of the Holy Spirit

4. Developing Vision
   Nurture Your Soul by Believing in Others and Their Growth

5. The Balancing Act
   Nurture Your Soul With Balance

6. The Big Adventure
   Nurture Your Soul With Risk

7. Collective Soul
   Nurture Your Soul Through Community

8. In Search of Sabbath
   Nurture Your Soul With a Commitment to Personal Renewal

My Favorite Books for Youth Workers

Better Safe Than Sued. Jack Crabtree. Loveland, CO: Group Publishing, Inc., 1998. A wealth of practical advice to keep youth workers off the thin ice of poor planning.

Boundaries. Drs. Henry Cloud and John Townsend. Grand Rapids, MI: Zondervan Publishing House, 1992. Many youth workers find themselves burned out. This excellent resource helps the reader learn to say "no."

Bringing Out the Best in People. Alan Loy McGinnis. Minneapolis, MN: Augsburg Publishing House, 1985. A positive, practical, and motivational book. A necessary resource for all leaders and managers.

Children Without Childhood. Marie Winn. NY: Pantheon Books, 1993. A penetrating look at our culture and how we rush children through childhood.

A Church for the 21st Century. Leith Anderson. Minneapolis, MN: Bethany House Publishers, 1992. A helpful prescription for the effective church and youth group in the new millennium.

Counseling Teenagers. Dr. G. Keith Olson. Loveland, CO: Group Publishing, 1984. A useful tool for counseling adolescents. Appropriate for volunteers and full-time youth workers.

Enjoy Your Middle Schooler. Wayne Rice. Grand Rapids, MI: Zondervan Publishing House, 1994. Six easy-to-read chapters on "The Wonder Years." Parents and youth workers discover key insights into the physical, emotional, social, intellectual, and spiritual development of young adolescents.

Family-Based Youth Ministry. Mark DeVries. Downers Grove, IL: InterVarsity Press, 1994. This book presents a thought-provoking challenge to include families in our youth ministry perspective.

Family Friendly Church. Ben Freudenburg. Loveland, CO: Group Publishing, 1998. This book outlines Ben's journey to equip families of youth in an effective home-based, church-supported youth ministry.

Family-Friendly Ideas Your Church Can Do. Loveland, CO: Group Publishing, 1998.

Fifty proven ideas for serving, learning, worshiping, and playing together. Very practical.

Help! I'm a Volunteer Youth Worker! Doug Fields. Grand Rapids, MI: Zondervan Publishing House, 1993. We give this book to each of our volunteers as a basic introduction to youth ministry. It offers fifty bite-size suggestions that are user-friendly and doable.

Helping the Struggling Adolescent. Les Parrott III, Grand Rapids, MI: Zondervan Publishing House, 1993. Describes thirty problems teenagers face and how you can help. This is a useful counseling aide, easy to use and comprehensive.

High School Ministry. Mike Yaconelli and Jim Burns. Grand Rapids, MI: Zondervan Publishing House, 1986. An insightful look at high school culture and how to have an impact on it. Specific strategies and activities are included.

How to Work With Rude, Obnoxious and Apathetic Kids. Les Christie. Wheaton, IL: Victor Books, 1994. Distracting, undisciplined teenagers can ruin a youth group. Learn how these problems can be opportunities to have a positive influence on the rowdy kids in your group.

In Search of Excellence. Thomas Peters and Robert H. Waterman, Jr. NY: Warner Books, 1982. The classic business book on excellence. I use it for discussions with our team on how we can develop excellence in youth work.

Junior High Ministry. Wayne Rice. Grand Rapids, MI: Zondervan Publishing House, 1998. The best book I am aware of on junior high ministry. Wayne Rice really understands the changes and challenges of early adolescence. Many pages of ideas make this book a very practical program resource.

My Utmost for His Highest. Oswald Chambers. Grand Rapids, MI: Discovery House Publishers, 1992. A classic, penetrating devotional.

New Directions for Youth Ministry. Loveland, CO: Group Publishing, Inc., 1998. Outlines ministry strategies and models that are working in real churches…with real kids…in the real world. Contributors are ministry veterans who are actually doing what they describe.

Principle-Centered Leadership. Stephen R. Covey. NY: Fireside Books, Simon & Schuster, Inc., 1992. Picking up where *The Seven Habits* leaves off, Covey develops the theme of character and leadership.

Pro-Teen Parent. Daniel M. Hahn. Sisters, OR: Questar Publishers, Inc., 1992. Ten practical and tested ways for parents and youth workers to encourage spiritual growth in teenagers.

Purpose-Driven Youth Ministry. Doug Fields. Grand Rapids, MI: Zondervan Publishing House, 1998. This is a primer for intentional youth ministry. It will help you build a balanced ministry.

Radical Christianity. Jim Burns. Ventura, CA: Regal Books, 1997. This is a useful resource for discipling youth to make a stand for Christ.

Radical Respect. (previously titled *Handling Your Hormones,* 1986). Jim Burns. Harvest House Publishers, Eugene, OR, 1991. My favorite resource for talking to teenagers about love and sexuality. A great resource for a course on sexuality.

The Seven Habits of Highly Effective People. Stephen R. Covey. NY: Simon & Schuster, Inc., 1989. Youth work is not simply a set of skills, but a matter of habits; of passion, principles, and patterns of behavior. Covey introduces seven habits that have relevant application to youth ministry.

Surviving Adolescence. Jim Burns. Ventura, CA: Regal Books, 1997. This book will help the youth worker influence teenagers to make positive choices and prevent them from making negative ones. Jim Burns challenges teenagers not to settle for second best. The study guide makes this a useful resource for group study and discussion.

Understanding Today's Youth Culture. Walt Mueller. Wheaton, IL: Tyndale House Publishers, 1994. This is a well-written and well-researched handbook for getting a grasp on today's teenagers and their culture.

User-Friendly Churches. George Barna. Ventura, CA: Regal Books, 1991. Evaluate how friendly your youth group is by learning from Barna about what makes groups/churches "friendly."

The Youth Worker's Handbook to Family Ministry. Chap Clark. Grand Rapids, MI: Zondervan Publishing House, 1997. This book is a guide to launching an intergenerational ministry and helping it grow.